What Made That Feel So [...]
Wells is a compelling ar[...]
to understand and heal [...]
with trauma-informed [...]
not only for individuals [...]
fessionals in the field of mental health, education, and beyond. I wholeheartedly recommend this book to our staff, clients, and partners as a guide to fostering resilience, understanding, and healing in the face of life's inevitable, complex challenges.

LANE SIMMONS

CEO and Clinical Advisor, the Trauma-Informed Care Training Center

What Made That Feel So Hard?: The Unstacking Method is an excellent book for anyone desiring to understand how the hardships in their past have impacted their life today. Each chapter offers real life examples to help the reader understand grief and how to unpack it. Questions at the end of each chapter help the reader if they are ready to engage the material at a deeper level. The book is well researched but is written in a way that is easily accessible. Wells uses personal anecdotes as well as evidence to help readers process past grief. Most importantly, the book offers hope and is a gift for those who have been burdened by grief.

DR. AMY HOYT

CEO of Mending Trauma

Whether the things we struggle with seem mundane or monstrous, *What Made That Feel So Hard?: The Unstacking Method* is a book guaranteed to have widespread impact and appeal. Lauren draws from personal experience, professional research and study, and countless hours of practical grief work with people of all ages to bring authenticity and earned fact to this volume. Her emphasis on curiosity and courage allows readers to begin unstacking the pebbles and rocks of trauma and grief that have collected in life without judgment. As a public health nurse and writer, I am beyond grateful to be able to recommend this book. Get yourself a copy today, and begin unstacking, knowing you are not alone. Together we can move forward with joy, strength and purpose.

MARILYN GARDNER
Director of Clinical & Cross-Cultural Training,
Author of *Between Worlds: Essays on Culture and Belonging*

Practical, hopeful, and deeply relatable - this book takes the complex topic of grief processing and makes it accessible through the weaving together of real life stories with scientific data. What I appreciate most, however, is the thoughtful and compassionate way in which Lauren encourages the reader to reflect on their own grief before helping others process theirs. Lauren's writing is like a warm hug and a supportive hand leading you through your own journey towards insight, self-compassion and healing.

MARIA TRICARICO
Therapist and owner of Amina TCK Therapy, LLC

This book offers a systematic approach to being kind to yourself. I didn't even realize how unkindly I was treating myself as I carried the weight of a wobbly tower until reading this book. Years of muscling through stuffed down pain, tormented by shame left me bitter, weary, and hopeless. Now, I have tools to live changed by those difficulties but no longer stunted by them. Beyond the methods, the compassion from the author seeps from the pages in her warm tone and comforting words. She invited me into a vulnerable space with a simple welcome mat not reserved for only the deepest traumas, nor just nice in theory but one that invited me to look objectively at past hurts in a way that urged me to be kind to myself through the process. This real and practical guide to unstacking my Grief Tower took me through the first steps in my journey of healing. In it, I found hope, relief, and renewed resilience.

ELENA

Whether you want to unstack a tall Grief Tower or help prevent one from forming in the first place, this is your book! Not only does Lauren give the tools to process your own grief and trauma, but she also shares the way in which we can come alongside children during their own hardships to keep their Grief Tower from stacking and then toppling in the first place. Lauren writes early on that "Compassion is not a limited resource reserved for only the 'really hard things.'" Any and all grief is worth processing in a healthy way, and this book is the path to do so. If you're a counselor or child educator, or a pastor, a parent or a friend, you must read this book. It will give you new and helpful language to use with anyone processing grief and trauma.

CATHERINE

LAUREN WELLS

What Made That Feel So Hard?

THE UNSTACKING METHOD

Stories of real people have been used throughout this book. However, names and personal characteristics have been changed in order to disguise their identities. Any resemblance to persons living or dead is purely coincidental and unintentional.

This book is heavily research-based and provides URLs within the footnotes for your use. Lauren Wells, Unstacking Company, and TCK Training are not responsible for, and should not be deemed to endorse or recommend, any website other than their own or any content available through the linked references.

What Made that Feel So Hard? The Unstacking Method
By Lauren Wells

Unstacking Company
Cohutta, Georgia
© 2024 Lauren Wells

ISBN: 979-8-218-36777-0

Edited by Elizabeth Trotter

To my girls, Clara and Audrey.

Your watching eyes fuel my desire to be
an example of how to navigate
the hard parts of life well.

CONTENTS

A Note from Lauren

I sent the draft of this book to my editor the week we discovered we were expecting our third child. With our girls in elementary school, we thought we were done with the baby stage. The discovery was followed shortly by, "We don't even have a crib anymore!," "But I really, really love sleeping through the night," and "This was not what I had planned!" My husband simply smiled and said, "But think of how many more grandchildren we're going to have!" There are forward thinkers, and then there's Aaron, who regularly jumps ahead twenty years.

The news came as a shock, but over the weeks I warmed up to the idea and shifted from skeptical to excited. As I battled daily nausea, I took comfort in lime-flavored popsicles and the fact that nausea is good because it means the baby is probably healthy. After several weeks, we shared the news with our girls, whose excitement was comparable to that of Christmas morning. They started a running list of names and shared the news with everyone they came across – including the checker at the grocery store.

Thanksgiving week, Aaron and I drove to the clinic for an ultrasound. With a growing belly and nausea still present that morning, we assumed everything was going well. It was not. "There's no heartbeat," the ultrasound technician said as we stared at our motionless baby on the screen. In shock, we were ushered into the next room to make the most awful decisions. Because it was Thanksgiving week and because of how far along I was, I ended up having surgery that day to remove the baby.

The day began with joy and a baby bump and ended with a flattened belly and so, so many tears.

It feels like a cruel twist of irony to have such an unexpected loss in the same season that I'm publishing a book on processing grief. It had been some time since my last major Grief Tower block, and I rather liked writing this book from a "been there, done that" past-tense perspective.

The funny thing about being a "grief expert" (a title often bestowed when someone else writes my bio), is that *knowing* all about how to process grief in healthy ways doesn't actually make hard things any easier.

I would greatly appreciate it if the tools I've spent years accumulating would take the hurt away and make hard things less painful.

I'd love to promise that what you will learn in these pages will make grief suck less. But I can tell you that's not true.

What I can tell you, is that the weeks between that awful day at the clinic and writing these words have been heartbreakingly painful. Watching my girls weep, packing up the maternity clothes I had just bought and hardly had the chance to wear, being continually reminded of the plans that were made that are now null and void, many nights of falling asleep on a tear-soaked pillow – it has been devastating.

I can also tell you that because of the innerwork and outward teaching I've been doing over the past decade, this season of grief has been navigated in ways my younger self wouldn't even recognize.

Having tools hasn't made it hurt less, but it has given me a map.

It has given me tools to unstack this gut-wrenching grief by:

- Knowing what normal looks like, so that when I am suddenly overwhelmed by sadness, when I'm physically exhausted, when I'm crankier than normal, when I'm wondering what's wrong with me, I can continually tell myself, "This is what grief looks like. I'm not crazy."

- Knowing what healthy coping looks like and recognizing when I'm slipping into unhealthy habits like sleeping or being overly busy to avoid feeling.
- Understanding that strength is not stuffing down the emotions and pushing through without a tear, like my younger self thought. Remembering that there is great strength in admitting that this is painful and letting myself experience the difficult emotions that I'd rather not.
- Knowing how to walk my kids through this grief in a way that allows them to name, feel, and recognize the sadness, anger, and pain that comes with such a loss.
- Having tools to unstack this Grief Tower block by giving time and space to process the reasons why this feels so hard.

As I wrote this book, I didn't expect that I would need my own words. I didn't expect that I would be the one working to actively unstack a block on my Grief Tower. As I gave this manuscript a final read-through, I didn't expect to want to throw it against the wall and devour these words all at the same time.

The Unstacking Method you'll learn in these pages doesn't make hard things feel less hard. But it does give tools for learning how to move through hard things in healthy ways – both the hard things that happened long ago that you didn't have tools to process well at the time and current hardships that you want to learn to navigate well.

So we're on this journey together. Join me in admitting that unstacking grief feels so hard and recognizing the strength in showing up anyway.

Introduction

I first wrote about the Grief Tower Model in my book, *The Grief Tower: A Practical Guide to Processing Grief with Third Culture Kids.* My expertise is working with expatriate families and, more specifically, their children — also known as Third Culture Kids, or TCKs. In 2019, I started a company called TCK Training to create research-based support and resources for these families and the organizations and companies who send them around the globe for business, foreign service, military, and humanitarian work. TCK Training rapidly grew as organizations and companies realized how interconnected longevity, performance, and well-being are to holistic family care – including care for the children.

It was in working with these families and adult TCKs (adults who lived globally mobile lives in their developmental years) to process past grief and trauma that I noticed a tendency to look at grief and trauma as isolated events. They wondered why *that* friend moving was such a big deal or why *this* evacuation seemed to change their child's behavior so drastically. What they didn't understand was that it wasn't just *that* friend or *that* evacuation; it was the fact that the grief of that friend moving was stacked on top of the past three friends who moved, the country relocation before that, the school change before that, and so on.

The analogy of a Grief Tower became a helpful way to illustrate the compounding effect of losses, especially when there wasn't time and space given for those losses to be grieved in the moment. The process of using the Grief Tower Model to process past grief became known as the Unstacking Method.

Over the years as the use of the Grief Tower Model grew in the expatriate community through books I had published on the subject and trainings and certifications TCK Training was offering, we began to hear of counseling practices, schools, and churches using the concept outside of the niche expatriate population. This led to the creation of The Unstacking Company, a company that teaches professionals, parents, pastors, leaders, school faculty – really anyone – how to use the concepts that came from the Grief Tower Model in their family, work, or community. Because while globally mobile families certainly have a lot of grief and loss, don't we all? We all have blocks on our Grief Tower. They may vary in size and scope, but that doesn't mean they aren't impactful.

As the Unstacking Company began to teach broader audiences about the Grief Tower, I knew that this book would need to be written.

The title question, *"What Made That Feel So Hard?"* is the best way I've found to get to the root of how a block on the Grief Tower has impacted our present. We all have current patterns and perspectives that are impacted by the harder parts of our story. When we learn to unstack our Grief Tower, we can look back at those hard things, investigate why they felt hard, and decide whether the things they taught us are worth carrying into the next part of our story.

This book invites you to be curious and courageous as you unstack your own Grief Tower and equips you to use the Unstacking Method to bring hope and healing to the people around you in formal or informal ways.

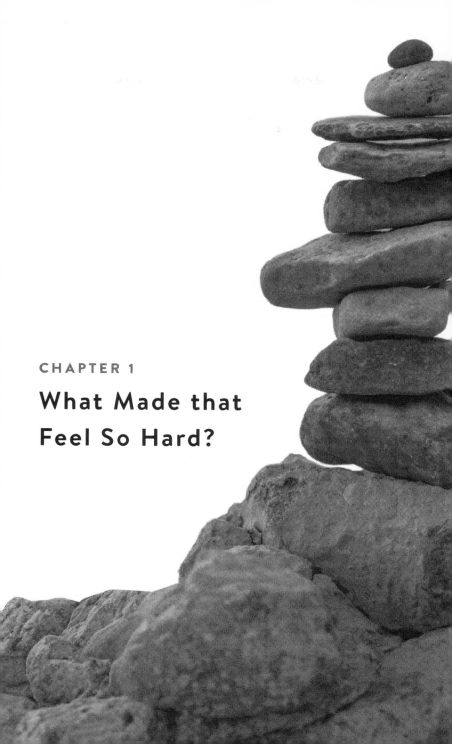

CHAPTER 1

What Made that Feel So Hard?

THE UNSTACKING METHOD

I stood in front of a crowd of college students. They stared at me, some sitting straight up with a pen and journal in hand, others slouching like a rag doll in an oversized hoodie, obviously only there because a friend dragged them along. With a pile of large wooden blocks in front of me, I began to share my life story. As I did, I stacked a block for each painful, traumatic, or difficult life event that I exposed to the crowd. One by one the tower stacked up taller and taller. A couple of times the tower teetered and a student would muffle, "Ooooh, here it goes!" But I kept on stacking.

By the time my story had covered my childhood and adolescence and reached my adult years, my block tower was on the verge of toppling. It swayed with each added block. Then I shared about my sophomore year in college, and the tower fell heavily with a loud crash, startling the slouching sleepers in the crowd (which, I'm not going to lie, was pretty satisfying). But I didn't stop there. I continued my story into adulthood, stacking the next blocks on top of the pile of crashed blocks, continuing to share one story after another, some traumatic, and some just difficult.

"This," I said, "is the story of my Grief Tower."

We all have hard things that happen in our developmental years (from birth to around age 25). I call these hard things "Grief Tower blocks." These blocks can be anything from the death of a beloved grandparent to growing up in an abusive home. When hard things happen in childhood, they are either processed through the loving and supportive care of an adult in our life (usually a parent), or they stack up because we didn't have nurture and support to help us grieve and make sense of the hardship.

As the tower stacks higher, we begin to find ways to cope with each new difficult experience. Sometimes these coping skills are healthy, and sometimes they grow into unhealthy coping skills; either way, they helped us survive. As the tower stacks, we also begin to decide, through the lens of the hardship, what we believe about ourselves, others, the world, and spirituality. Each new hard thing that comes our way tends to subconsciously confirm whatever our previous grief blocks taught us.

Unstacking is the process of being curious about how our past hardships have influenced how we live our present life. It's the process of feeling the emotions that perhaps we didn't allow ourselves to – or didn't know how to – when that hard thing happened. It's investigating how that difficult thing made us think about ourselves and act in relationships. It's recognizing that the things we're doing today that are holding us back from thriving might be because we're carrying a tower of grief that was never unstacked along the way. Unstacking is being brave enough to pick up your grief blocks and start asking questions.

WHY UNSTACK IT?

Do It for Yourself
Are there patterns in your life that you don't like? Do you have unhelpful thoughts that you ruminate on or addictive behaviors that you can't seem to kick? The reason these patterns and thoughts can have such a grip on you is because they're most likely connected to something that happened in the past.

What happened in the past taught your brain and body some truths or understanding about the world. In the present, your brain and body act on instinct based on what they "know" about the way the world works. We might see the symptoms of unhelpful patterns – the need for constant approval, the failed relationships, the constant anxiety – but we need to do some excavating in order to get to the root of those patterns.

Digging deeper allows us to heal the part of our brain that decided that thought or action was the necessary response to the hard thing we experienced. But that doesn't always mean that the Grief Tower block *feels* like it needs healing. Stephanie Foo, in her incredible memoir about healing from Complex-PTSD, says, "Just because the wound doesn't hurt doesn't mean it's healed. If it looks good and it feels good, it should be all good, right? But over the years I'd smoothed perfect white layers of spackle over gaping structural holes."[1]

Without doing the work of unstacking, you might stay stuck in unhealthy or harmful patterns that are connected to hard things that may or may not *feel* hard. Unstacking allows you to examine your story so that you can see if there are things from your past holding you back from living the fullest life possible.

For these reasons alone it's important to unstack the Grief Tower. We want to see how learned beliefs and responses have impacted our life today. But it's also important because unresolved grief doesn't only impact our mental and relational well-being. The Grief Tower can only grow so tall before it crashes and our body responds. In Chapter 6 we'll look at the symptoms of a crashed Grief Tower and how we can prevent the crash or heal from it. Our bodies weren't meant to carry the weight of unprocessed grief and will only let you ignore your Grief Tower for so long before crying out in ways you're forced to pay attention to.

Do It for Your Relationships

Our patterns have a huge influence on the people closest to us – our family, friends, and loved ones. In order to love these people well, we have to be aware of what our past hardships have taught us about ourselves and about relationships. When you aren't aware of relational beliefs or patterns that you're living into, or you are aware but can't seem to stop the harmful pattern, you won't be able to bring your healthiest self into a

---

1 Foo, S. (2022). p. 111. *What my bones know: a memoir of healing from complex trauma* (1st ed.). Ballantine Group.

relationship. Because we know that relationships are a critical part of holistic health, it's worth exploring how past pain might be impacting the way you show up in relationships today.

Do It for Your Great-Great-Grandkids

One of the most fascinating and motivating factors of healing past hurt is the science of epigenetics – the study of how the things that have happened to you affect the expression of your genes.

A group of researchers at Emory University investigated the hypothesis that trauma in one generation can affect DNA, and thus, the impact of the trauma can be passed down from one generation to the next. In this study, they took a group of mice and administered a cherry scent with a simultaneous electric shock. Before long, the mice's brains would flood with stress chemicals when they smelled the cherry scent, even if there was no accompanying shock. We would call this being "triggered." Their brains and bodies were responding to stimuli that reminded them of past trauma.

After these mice had baby mice, the scientists administered the same cherry scent to this next generation. These mice had never experienced a shock, yet their brains responded with the same triggered response. The same experiment was done on the children of those mice (the grandchildren of the original mice) with the same outcome. The original mice experienced the trauma, and two generations later their grandchildren experienced the same triggered response to the same stimulus. They also found in this study that the DNA-encoded trauma response could be passed down through the mother or the father.[2]

This is why we hear things like, "I should stay away from alcohol because my father and grandfather were alcoholics" or, "My family has a history of depression and suicide." It's not

2 Dias, B. Ressler, K. (2013). Parental olfactory experience influences behavior and neural structure in subsequent generations. *Nature Neuroscience,* 17(1).

only that a person was exposed to certain environments but also that certain biological responses can attach to our DNA and pass down generation to generation.

But here's the incredible news: these genetic codes can be changed! When we heal from past trauma, we not only undo the imprinted genetic code, but we create new genetic codes that are more resilient to hardship and trauma. This means that we can literally pass down resilience and stop passing down the imprints of generational trauma to future generations.

I remember learning about this years ago, shortly after my two children were born and before I'd done the bulk of my healing, and thinking frustratedly, "Well, that was a greatly missed opportunity. Can't rewrite their genes now."

Fortunately, we may still have the opportunity to help our children (and even grandchildren) heal. The Unstacking Method actually began with children, teaching vulnerable youth the importance of, and tools for, processing hard things as they come. By doing our own unstacking, and by guiding the children in our lives to process their Grief Tower, we can be a catalyst for shifting their DNA code through the proactive healing done throughout their life. Even though after they're born we can't modify our children's DNA internally through changing the genetic codes in our body, we *can* externally influence a change in their genetic code through how we guide, support, and care through difficult emotions and circumstances. Chapter 15 will give tools for doing this well.

USING THIS BOOK

This book will guide you through processing your own Grief Tower first and then offer tools for helping others to unstack theirs. Chapters 2 through 11 will educate you on the various components of the Unstacking Method and guide you to begin reflecting. Chapter 13 walks you through the Unstacking

Method. Whether we're using the Unstacking Method preventively or reactively, the process is the same:

- List the blocks on your Grief Tower by creating a Grief Tower Timeline (all the memorable hardships that happened in your developmental years)

This list becomes your Processing To-Do List. Then, one by one you'll:

- Investigate how each block impacted your internal narratives (your beliefs about yourself, others, the world, and spirituality)
- Discover which coping skills you learned to use and when
- Name and feel the emotions of each grief block
- Learn how your Grief Tower has served you and identify the strengths that trace back to your grief blocks

Chapter 15 offers tools and insight for using the method with children, and Chapter 16 provides suggestions for using the Unstacking Method with adults in a professional setting.

This method has been successfully used by individuals doing their own processing, as well as by school counselors, trauma therapists, social workers treating at-risk youth, life coaches, pastoral counselors, parents with their own children, and more. If you opened this book for the purpose of helping others, I understand the temptation to skip to the final chapters of this book. Please don't. What I have found in teaching this methodology to thousands is that first working through your own unstacking is not only the best way to learn the process, but it can also bring up your own patterns and narratives in ways that even years of counseling may not have brought to light.

So pull out a dedicated notebook or journal and get ready to begin the process of unstacking your Grief Tower.

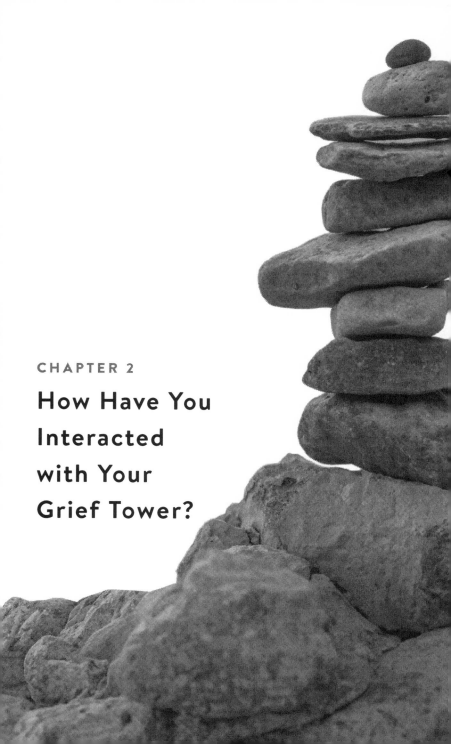

CHAPTER 2

How Have You Interacted with Your Grief Tower?

What do you think of when you hear the word "grief"? Most of us think of death. While that is certainly one of the causes of grief, the term is so much more broad than that. You may have deaths on your Grief Tower, but you likely have more of what could be perceived as smaller, less significant blocks on your tower – a good friend who moved away, a lost job, a move to a new city, a breakup, etc. These events still fit the definition of grief, in that you are losing someone or something that was important to you, but they often don't get the attention of the bigger "blocks" like death or violence.

What I've found in helping hundreds of families and individuals unstack their Grief Towers is that it's usually these "smaller" blocks that have the biggest grip on our life. This is because as these hardships happen throughout our life, they don't seem to warrant the attention and processing that the big things do. We typically give time and attention to grieving a death, but a lost job doesn't seem to deserve the same attentiveness. What happens, then, is that the little things keep going unprocessed, and the tower keeps growing taller and taller. On their own, each of those experiences may not have been that significant, but on top of several other difficult things, the impact increases.

As the tower stacks, so do our beliefs about the world, our role in relationships, and our perspective on spirituality. And these beliefs influence our actions. Before we know it, we are thinking and operating out of our Grief Tower. More than that, our tall tower begins to affect our physical well-being, which we'll explore more throughout this book. Trauma researcher, Dr. Amy Hoyt, says, "It is normal to want to avoid remembering our past trauma. Unfortunately, our body will stay stuck in the fight/flight/or freeze response until we address it. Eventually we have to face what we are avoiding, or the body will suffer. The body never forgets."[3]

---

3 Hoyt, Amy. [@mendingtrauma]. (2023, August 24)

These blocks that stack on our tower can be referred to in a number of ways. You might label them as trauma, grief, hardship, difficult experiences, or another term. I've found that referring to them as "blocks" can take away the need to get caught up in labels, though throughout the book, I'll refer to them using all of those terms interchangeably.

GETTING CURIOUS

As I've been working on this book, friends and acquaintances have asked me what it's about. When I give them my short elevator pitch, I sometimes get responses like, "I'm not sure I want to know what's on *my* Grief Tower!" or, "Yeah, there's probably a lot of stuff back there, but that seems like a lot of work to dig it all up."

Often our subconscious reason for not getting curious is because it feels vulnerable. Opening up past hurts, exposing unhealthy patterns, looking deep into the hardest parts of our story – it all feels a bit like jumping into deep, dark water. That feels uncomfortable at best and sometimes just downright terrifying.

But, as Brené Brown says, "Vulnerability is not weakness; it's our most accurate measure of courage."[4]

I've worked with courageous teenage boys who dove into the deep water to unstack their Grief Tower so that they could move forward healthier. And I've worked with grown men who have said, "Yeah, I'm not going there. My tower is just fine how it is."

Courageous curiosity seems to be the number one indicator of whether someone will work through the unstacking process or not.

---

4 Brown, B. (2017). *Braving the wilderness: The quest for true belonging and the courage to stand alone.* Random House.

PLAYING THE ROLE OF INVESTIGATOR

Working with children and teens has meant that I'm often facilitating unstacking with people who are forced to be there. Sometimes they are willing participants, and sometimes they make it perfectly clear that they would rather be doing anything else. But if I can get them curious, I can get them unstacking.

By playing the role of the investigator, we can start to answer the questions:

- Why do I do that?
- Why do I think that way?
- Why can't I get over this?
- Why am I like that?
- Why can't I stop doing that?
- Why does this keep happening?
- Why does that still feel so hard?

If you're not curious, investigate that. Why don't you feel curious? Is it fear? Ambivalence? A hard thing from your past that taught you it wasn't safe? The answers to these questions might be the reasons you've avoided your Grief Tower.

Another significant reason you may not have unstacked your tower along the way is that you haven't had people in your life to teach you how to process difficult things and provide you with comfort and support through grief and loss, especially in your childhood. When children go through difficult experiences, they should have caring adults teaching them how to name and feel emotions, showing them what comfort and support should look like, and planting helpful narratives such as, "You are strong and brave." Did you have that support growing up? If not, what were the messages you heard around emotions or getting through difficult experiences?

Investigate how the messaging you received or the comfort

and support you did or did not receive has influenced how you approach this idea of unstacking your Grief Tower.

IGNORING YOUR GRIEF TOWER

There are many reasons other than avoiding vulnerability or childhood messages around emotions that we may ignore blocks on our Grief Tower. Here are some of the most common:

It's not as bad if it happens to everyone. There is a strange phenomenon that takes place when a group experiences a difficulty at the same time. The shared nature of the experience causes everyone to consciously or subconsciously disallow themselves to grieve because "we're all going through it." This certainly happened during the COVID-19 pandemic. When debriefing dozens of families who were evacuated from countries around the world in 2020, I regularly heard, "Yeah, that was hard, but I can't feel too sad. Everyone else is going through the same thing." The permission for it to feel hard and to be treated as such seemed to dissipate in light of the communal nature of the tragedy.

The truth is, something can happen to everyone *and* still feel extremely difficult for each person and warrant the emotions that come with devastation. Communally pushing down grief doesn't make it go away; it just makes everyone's towers grow simultaneously and invites shame on those who *are* doing the good work of grieving.

Ultimately it was for the best! I often hear sentiments like, "It was hard, but look at all the good things that came from it!" All the optimistic, positive-energy people start to sheepishly grin here.

There is absolutely space to recognize the redemptive parts of a difficult experience, but only focusing on the end of the story doesn't give space for grieving the emotions that were felt before you knew all the good that would come from it. Some of the most impactful blocks that I've seen on Grief Towers are those that were skipped past in an effort to focus on the good. If you're in this "but it all turned out well in the end" camp, it may feel pointless and uncomfortable to look back at difficult experiences that had a happy ending and focus on the difficult emotions of that experience.

I understand because that's how I'm wired too. (This may surprise you since I somehow became an expert on processing grief, but I digress.) Here's what I've learned: looking back doesn't mean betraying the part of you that wants and needs to hold onto the positive pieces of those memories. It means going back and doing the work of examining that block on your tower to see if there might be pieces of it that are impacting your life in ways that aren't helpful. It's picking it up to make sure that it actually is unstacked and isn't a block that's adding to the height of your tower. That way it can truly be "for the best" because there aren't any lingering unprocessed pieces hiding down deep.

It's not as bad as what others have gone through. When you know people whose lives have been so much more grief-filled than yours, it may be easy to ignore your own difficult experiences because, compared to those of others, yours isn't very significant. But here's the thing: you're not processing their Grief Tower. You're processing yours. Yes, they may have a tall Grief Tower filled with grief and trauma, and it will impact them. You, however, also have a Grief Tower filled with difficult experiences that will impact you. Compassion is not a limited resource reserved for only the "really hard things." There is enough compassion to go around and to warrant the attention of unstacking your Grief Tower even if what's on it seems minute in comparison to someone else's.

I had to stuff down so I could step up. Perhaps you've found yourself playing the role of caretaker, comforter, or even mediator. During difficult events or seasons, the people around you were also not doing well, and you felt it was your responsibility to care for them. While anyone can experience this, I've seen that it tends to disproportionately be the firstborn of the family who adopts this role. Unfortunately, these childhood roles don't often change naturally in adulthood; the caretaking just expands from the family of origin to other people in their adult life. If your lack of unstacking is because you stuffed down your emotions to step up for your parents, your siblings, or your own children, your grief still needs to be processed. Continuing to meet the emotional needs of others at the expense of your own isn't a sustainable solution. You can be loving, caring, and supportive *and* still do your own unstacking.

It is "normal." Some difficult experiences are so common that we don't allow ourselves to feel and process the emotions that came with them. What is "normal" depends on your community. In some communities the divorce of parents is commonplace, so perhaps as a child you heard or thought, "All of my friends' parents are divorced, so it's not a big deal that my parents are getting divorced now too." In the expatriate community evacuations are common. Families are given 24-48 hours' notice to pack up their lives and leave the country, often never to return. I've debriefed families who at some point experienced an evacuation, and when I mentioned it as a block on their family's tower, I was told, "It's a really normal part of diplomat life, so it's not really a big deal." Unfortunately, normalizing the grief experience doesn't unstack it; it only keeps it on our tower.

It was so long ago. Some blocks on your Grief Tower may have been collecting dust for a long time. You may be skeptical that experiences that happened so long ago could impact your adulthood and current reality. What I am constantly amazed by, however, is the undeniable impact that Grief Tower blocks, especially those that were stacked during our childhood, have on how we live out our lives. As you go through this process of unstacking, you may be amazed to see how much weight your tower has covertly carried in your life.

It is or has been dismissed by people in your life. I was debriefing a teenager, and he briefly mentioned something difficult that happened when he was a child. I said, "That sounds like a block on your Grief Tower!" He said, "Nah, my mom said it wasn't a big deal." You may have had a parent, friend, spouse, or someone else in your life shut you down in the past, making you feel that something you thought was difficult wasn't actually worthy of grief. As you begin to look at your Grief Tower, be conscientious of any block that you hesitate to add to your tower because someone dismissed it as insignificant. It is your tower to process, and if you felt that experience was hard, then it deserves to be processed.

It's exhausting and time consuming. Setting aside time and energy to look at the hardest parts of our lives and dig into them like we're archeologists with an incredibly depressing mission can easily be pushed down the to-do list. If you're like me, to-do list items that don't sound easy or inspiring seem to stay on your to-do list eternally (hence my ever-growing mountain of laundry). Taking time to unstack your Grief Tower is probably something you'll have to muster up willpower to do. You may find yourself mentally, emotionally, and physically exhausted after working through a block. You may think, "I've hardly done anything today, so why am I so tired?" I don't have to tell you that it's worth doing anyway — if you're reading this book, I assume you know that. But I do want to acknowledge and validate the fact that this work isn't easy and that it may feel worse before it gets better.

THE FLIP SIDE

Some of us don't ignore our Grief Tower. In fact, we know our Grief Tower well and have perhaps even taken pride in its height and sturdiness. For those in this camp, here are the most common reasons for not ignoring, but also not unstacking.

Ruminating. Instead of doing the good work of processing the hard things, we instead hold onto that past hurt and pain with a death grip that won't let go. We think about it often, maybe talk about it often, and no matter how much we do of either of those, the pain doesn't go away. Ruminating is like a hula hoop, and processing is like a slinky. When we're processing something difficult that has happened, we'll need to think, talk, create, and tell the story for a while until the pain slowly eases and we can move forward. If you follow the curves of a slinky with your finger, you'll eventually get to the end because the circular motion is making forward progress as you go round and round.

But if you trace your finger around a hula hoop, you'll see that you could do that an infinite number of times. That's ruminating. It's staying stuck in how the Grief Tower block has impacted you without ever moving forward toward health and healing. If you've felt stuck going round and round the hula hoop, the Unstacking process will guide you in understanding what forward progress does and does not look like and will teach you how to move forward.

Musing. I once had a client say, "I'm worried that if I unstack my Grief Tower, I won't have anything to write music about anymore. The sadness and pain are my muse." Sometimes our grief has led to creative inspiration or even feels like part of our identity. We like what the sadness and moodiness have done for us. We like the emotional weight we carry. But what many people have found is that the depth of healthy authenticity that comes from unstacking and healing a tall Grief Tower brings just as much inspiration and also doesn't change you into the happy-go-lucky person that you're not. Unstacking doesn't take away your emotional depth or awareness. Instead, it invites you toward deep healing that allows you to feel your emotions while also intellectually investigating the blocks on your tower and deciding which parts are healthy and which are unhealthy to you and those around you.

Protecting. "But I don't want to forget how hard that was. That feels like betrayal." Sometimes it can feel like unstacking the Grief Tower reduces the significance of what happened. It can feel like you're betraying someone or trying to minimize how impactful that hard thing has been. It makes sense that you would want to protect your Grief Tower and the significance of what's on it. But healing does not mean forgetting. Unstacking doesn't mean getting over it. It means finding a new, healthier version of yourself that has been imprinted by the difficult thing that happened.

BEING A SAFE SPACE FOR YOURSELF

Shut Down Responses

At Unstacking Company we often teach about being a safe space. The majority of this session is spent talking about "shutdown responses" vs. "safe space responses." While we're usually talking about these for the purpose of teaching participants how to be a safe space for others, it is an important principle for responding well to ourselves when we've experienced something difficult. You may have used these shut down responses as a way to avoid experiencing the emotions that accompanied the blocks on your Grief Tower. You may also be tempted to use them as you begin the process of unstacking. Knowing what they are and how to change your internal language is an important part of the processing work.

When we use shutdown responses on ourselves, we're using them to keep from feeling or exploring a difficult emotion or sometimes from even admitting that the experience *was* difficult.

The most common shutdown responses are:

DOWNPLAYING – convincing yourself that it's not worthy of a difficult emotion because it wasn't that serious.

> *"It wasn't that big of a deal."*
> *"I shouldn't be feeling so ____."*

DEFENDING – defending the reason for your difficult emotion. There can be a good, legitimate reason for what happened, *and* it can still hurt. Good intention can still have a harmful impact, and that impact is what needs to be processed.

> *"There was probably a good reason for it."*
> *"I'm sure they were doing the best they could."*
> *"I know they didn't intend to hurt me."*

COMPARING – not allowing emotion because it wasn't as bad as something bigger you've gone through or something someone else has experienced. I'll say it again: compassion is not a limited resource. When we compare to decide if we should allow ourselves to express the difficult emotion, we're saying that compassion should be given based on how our situation compares to someone else's or how one block of ours compares to another. But the reality is, compassion is not in scarce supply, and there's enough to go around for our big and our small things, for our hard things and their hard things.

> *"Others have had it so much worse."*
> *"This doesn't even come close to the time when..."*

CORRECTING – telling yourself to turn off the emotions once you've learned that the facts were different than you thought. This often happens when we're exploring a difficult situation that happened during childhood and we learn more details than we knew at the time.

> *"Now that I know the whole story, those feelings should go away."*
> *"I don't know why I'm still feeling this way even though I know it all worked out in the end."*
> *"Why won't my feelings listen to the facts!?"*

As you work through this book, being aware of shutdown responses can help you to catch yourself and show up with a safe space response instead.

Safe space responses are:

ACKNOWLEDGING – acknowledging to yourself that feeling emotions when you're processing grief blocks is good, healthy, and takes a lot of courage.

> *"It's okay to feel difficult emotions about things that happened in the past."*
> *"Letting myself think about those grief blocks is good and healthy."*
> *"I'm allowed to experience emotions, even about things that happened long ago, and to find people who can walk with me through it."*
> *"This is hard work, but I know it's worth it."*

AFFIRMING – giving yourself validation that what happened was hard and that you're allowed to feel that way even if you know details now that you didn't know then or you know that things turned out ok.

> *"It makes sense that that would've felt hard."*
> *"They had good intentions, but it still hurt me."*

"It was a big deal to me."
"I hate that that happened."
"That wasn't how it was supposed to be."
"That should have never happened to me."

COMFORTING – seeking out a hug, snuggling under a cozy blanket, eating a favorite snack, drinking a glass of water or cup of tea, taking a walk, calling a good friend. Give yourself permission to be comforted when you're experiencing emotions from things that happened long ago. Your brain may know that it was a long time ago, but your body and emotions may be responding as they did when that hard thing first happened. Give yourself grace for that response, and seek comfort when you need it.

THE WHY

An important exercise to do before continuing on with this process is to choose a few "whys" for doing this work. This is equally important for those of us who have ignored our Grief Tower and those of us who have clung to it. Perhaps you are unstacking your Grief Tower so that you can help others unstack theirs, and you know that you can't lead someone where you haven't been. Perhaps you've realized that holding onto unprocessed grief is impacting your relationships or your mental health.

Maybe you're just curious about how your Grief Tower has impacted your current life. Or you know that your past grief has kept you stuck, and you're ready to be free from the weight of that. Perhaps you want to parent your children in a way that helps them process grief along the way so that they don't have a tall tower to deal with in adulthood. Or maybe you know that you don't want to pass the impact of your Grief Tower down to your children and grandchildren. Whatever the reason, I encourage you to take a moment to list one to three "whys" that will keep you motivated on this processing journey.

Exercise #1: Have you historically ignored or ruminated on your Grief Tower?

If you tend to ignore it, which of the reasons that I mentioned have you used for not processing the difficult things that have happened in your life?

If you tend to ruminate, what is your mindset behind the rumination?

Exercise #2: Thinking about the common shutdown responses of downplaying, defending, comparing, and correcting, which do you tend to use most to shut yourself down from admitting and/or experiencing emotion?

Exercise #3: What are your "whys"? Who are you doing this work for? What do you hope will happen? How do you hope your life will change because of it?

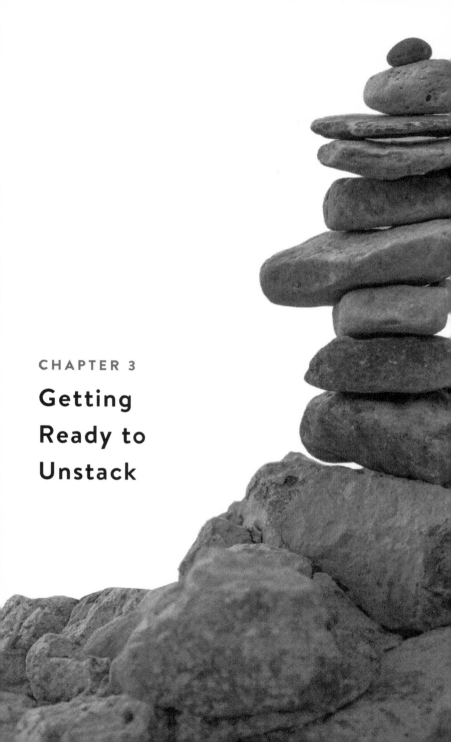

CHAPTER 3

Getting Ready to Unstack

BEGINNING THE PROCESS

You've probably noticed by now that this isn't a light-hearted read. Maybe this book is feeling increasingly heavier in your hands. The unstacking process isn't easy, and it's important to acknowledge that and give yourself permission for it to feel hard.

- **You might feel more difficult emotions than you typically do as you work through this book**. For some of you, that may feel uncomfortable. Notice when your body responds to what you're reading, and give yourself permission to feel that response.
- **You might need to take breaks.** You might read this book straight through, working through your Grief Tower and hunting for internal narratives with ease. But more likely, you'll need to pause along the way and give your body and brain a break. After engaging in this book, it can be helpful to allow your brain to focus on something completely different. This could include getting lost in a fiction novel, watching a TV show or movie, listening to a podcast, or spending lighthearted time with a friend.
- **Find ways to comfort yourself.** Wrapping yourself in a soft blanket, drinking tea from your favorite mug, lighting candles, going to the gym, taking a bath – do whatever helps your body to relax.
- **Allow yourself to indulge a little in your favorite foods or treats.** I joke with my husband that I can't process grief without dark chocolate. Allowing that small comfort has become a gift to myself while doing the hard work of processing.
- **Make nap/rest time a priority.** This work is more physically draining than you may imagine. Give yourself permission to get extra rest. Sleep in, take a nap, go to bed early. Listen to your body when it tells you to sleep.

- **Find others who can journey with you.** These may be people with whom you share details of your Grief Tower, or they may be friends to whom you simply say, "I'm working through a book right now that's bringing up some heavy things. Could you please check in with me/get lunch with me/do something fun with me/pray for me over the next couple of weeks?" Don't allow pride to keep you from asking for support from the people who love you.

As you engage in this process, be kind to yourself. It is not easy work, and doing it without the permissions above doesn't mean you are an overachiever. You cannot get an "A" in grief processing. No one is evaluating your performance or your ability to process grief. There is no grade, no winner, no way to do this impressively. Give yourself the grace and permission for this to feel hard and for you to act accordingly.

PUSHING PAUSE

As with any deep internal work, it's important to have a plan for additional support if you need it and to determine clear indicators of when you need it. This Unstacking Method purposefully brings up difficult things from the past. Some people find that they are able to work through the method on their own, reaching out to supportive friends or family when they need to verbally process or be comforted. Some people, however, find that digging into their past brings up pain and emotions that need a professional counselor's support.

Knowing when to push pause requires *listening to your body.* I remember hearing the phrase, "listen to your body," in my early twenties and thinking it was a bunch of fluffy woowoo for people who also had dreamcatchers, used words like "zen" and "aura," and preached the immense benefits of a good yoga flow. I wasn't convinced that my body and emotions were very interconnected, and if they were, ignoring it seemed like the more efficient option.

And then I began working with grieving children. I had developed a pre-departure training program for the organization I was working with, and I was regularly teaching children and teens who were getting ready to transition to a new country. Our training program was often their last stop before getting on the airplane, so they were coming in fresh from saying "goodbye" to their friends, home, school, and former life. Part of the program involved talking about grief and the losses that come with leaving your culture, friends, and home to go start life in an entirely new world.

For one of the lessons, we played a game where the children would hunt for Easter eggs and then bring them all back to the circle. Inside each egg was a slip of paper with an example of a "hidden loss" and a piece of candy to make this depressing game seem almost enjoyable. One by one, the children and teens would open the egg, eat the candy, and read the "hidden loss."

As they read slips that said things like, "my best friend having a new best friend," "not having my favorite holiday foods," "not seeing my grandparents for a long time," or "not feeling known in the new place," I would watch their reactions. Most of the time, there were some tears in the group as we kept putting words to the grief and anticipated loss they were experiencing. This game often facilitated some wonderfully deep processing discussions and helped the children to have language for, and not feel alone in, their grief.

But every once in a while, I would see something shift in one of the kids. I would notice their body tense up or begin to shake, or they'd begin to get extremely fidgety. Their body was visibly responding to the experience of naming these losses. Once, a teenage boy got up and raged outside. Another time, a shaky girl retreated to the bathroom. The fidgety boy said, "I'm done talking about this. I need to do something else. NOW."

We'll talk in Chapter 15 ("Using the Grief Tower with Children") about what psychiatrist, Dr. Dan Siegel calls the "window of tolerance" and how to notice if children have moved outside of it and need to stop processing. But we adults also have a window of tolerance – a point at which our body says, "Nope, I'm done!" – and we need to listen to it and stop.

Listening to your body looks very similar to what I was doing with the children in those groups. It's noticing if something shifts or changes and being willing to change direction or stop entirely in response to your body.

Some common reactions to look for are:

- Feeling suddenly antsy (fidgeting, bouncing, feeling like you can't sit still)
- A racing or abnormally beating heart
- Sweating
- Dissociating (feeling like you're outside your body)
- Feeling emotionally numb or shut down
- Seeing stars/feeling like you're going to pass out
- Feeling sick to your stomach
- An uncontrollable emotional response such as rage or intense sobbing
- Any thoughts of self-harm or suicide
- Feelings of panic

If you experience these, it means you've pushed your brain past what it is ready to handle. That doesn't mean that you should never process that block again, but it does mean that you should:

- Take a break and regulate
  - » Drink a glass of water
  - » Take some deep breaths
  - » Go for a walk
  - » Take a shower

> » Breathe in for 5 seconds and out for 8 seconds
> » Go outside barefoot
> » Wrap yourself tightly with a blanket
- Push pause on processing the specific block that caused that reaction and find a mental health professional to help you process it.
- Call a crisis hotline (USA - 988, Canada - 1-833-456-4566, Quebec 1-866-277-3553) if you need immediate support or feel that you're a danger to yourself or others.

A major benefit of the Unstacking Model is that you're looking at one block at a time. This makes it possible to pause processing one block but still continue to work through some of the others. There may be some blocks that you're able to process on your own or with a trusted friend and others that you discover need to be put to the side and taken to a mental health professional to process. I've had many clients share that it was helpful for them to have sorted out the blocks ahead of time. They could show up to therapy knowing what they needed help to process.

As you work through this book, and for some of you, as you think about using the Unstacking Model with others, it's important to pay attention to what your body (or theirs) is doing in response to processing. Tears and other forms of emotional expression are normal, healthy, and good. But intense dysregulation, like the examples above, should signal you to press pause, to cope, and to set that specific block aside for now.

SUPPORT

I pray that your current close relationships are with people who desire to understand the hard parts of your story and who don't dismiss your grief, but I know the reality is that's not always the case. If you are in a relationship with someone who uses one of the reasons in this chapter to discount your grief or discourage you from taking the time to do the work of processing your Grief Tower, I would encourage you to gracefully continue on through this work, knowing that it is not only important and healthy for you to do so, but that it will also allow you to be a healthier person in those relationships.

If you find that you're not being met with supportive responses or that the people around you habitually give shutdown responses, I would encourage you to find someone who can show up as an emotionally safe space as you work through the unstacking process. This could be a friend or even a paid counselor.

Having a supportive person or community beside you as you begin to unstack your Grief Tower is an important piece of walking through this process well.

Exercise #1: Which regulation tools seem like they would work best for you if you were to experience a physical reaction that would require you to regulate your body?

Exercise #2: Who are the supportive people in your life who have proven to be safe and trustworthy when you share difficult things?

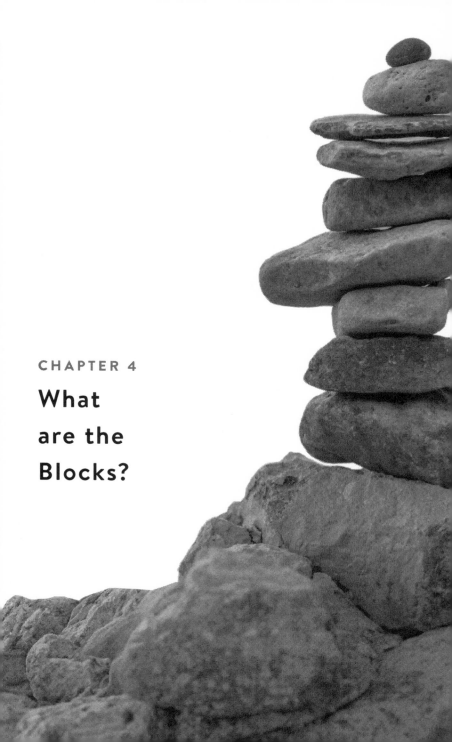

CHAPTER 4

What
are the
Blocks?

A few years ago, a sixty-nine-year-old man sat in Unstacking Sessions. Like all of my clients at that time, he had grown up in a globally mobile family, moving to a different country every two to three years of his childhood. These adventures had shaped his life in many positive, rewarding ways, granting him adaptability, a deeply broad perspective, and the ability to navigate unfamiliar cultures and languages with relative ease.

But alongside these world traveling perks was stacked a tower of constant loss – the continuous goodbyes to people, places, languages, and entire worlds. In those scarce seasons of stability when he wasn't relocating, the incredibly transient expatriate community meant that everyone else was. Best friends moved away, never to be seen again. Favorite teachers left part way through the school year. Events that he had been dreaming about and looking forward to were canceled because the people who had planned them left unexpectedly.

Each of these losses or difficult experiences seemed manageable or even insignificant on their own, but when they kept coming and the tower of stacked losses kept growing, it began to impact his view of himself, others, the world, and even God.

As we spent our sessions holding and exploring each block on his tower, he began to mine the messages and beliefs that felt deeply true to his core. "It's not safe to get close to people; they always leave," "I have to be strong for the people around me," and "God either isn't real, or if he is, he must not care about me."

As he reflected on his adult life, he realized he'd been living deeply into these narratives for the past five decades. He had never been married; he could name many friends who considered him a close friend but none whom he felt close to; and he had never lived in one place for longer than three years. As we began to unpack the impact of his Grief Tower, he said, "I cannot believe I've let my Grief Tower run my life all these years. That ends today."

WHAT ARE THE BLOCKS?

To put it simply, your Grief Tower consists of anything that has happened during your life that felt particularly difficult. For the purpose of the unstacking process that you'll walk through in this book, you'll focus only on the Grief Tower blocks from your developmental years (birth to around 25 years old).

The reason we focus on the developmental years is because it is in those years that we are developing narratives about ourselves, others, the world, and spirituality. It is also during those years that the increase of the stress hormone, cortisol, wreaks the most havoc on our growing brain. While difficult things certainly happen after age 25, those later blocks tend to confirm the narratives that were already there from the developmental years. However, there is no limit to processing. If there is something significant that happened later in life that you'd like to add to your Grief Tower for processing, you are welcome to do so.

It can be helpful to think of the types of small "t" and big "T" traumas that might be blocks on your Grief Tower in categories. The categories are there to help you brainstorm your Grief Tower blocks, but if there is something that doesn't fit squarely in one of the categories, don't be afraid to put it on your tower anyway. Categorizing is meant to be a helpful tool, not a one-size-fits-all box.

Losses

The first category is broad: losses. Losses can be both obvious and hidden. I like to think of the obvious losses as the first layer. These are the things that people point out as losses, and they are the broadest category. Examples include losing a loved one, moving, changing schools, a friend moving away, parents divorcing. When you're creating your Grief Tower Timeline in Chapter 13, the obvious losses are what you will put on there as blocks.

It is important to acknowledge, however, that there is a sublayer of losses, often referred to as hidden losses. These are the elements underneath the obvious loss that explain why that loss feels so hard.

Hidden losses are often neither obvious nor acknowledged, but if we identify them, they can put words to our grief. Hidden losses often go unnoticed by those who haven't gone through a similar experience, which is why it can sometimes feel difficult to communicate the extent of your grief. The obvious loss may not appear significant, but when you consider the associated hidden losses, you can understand why it would be an influential block on your Grief Tower.

These hidden losses could be:

- Loss of being known
- Loss of routine
- Loss of knowing what's expected of you
- Loss of your status
- Loss of being able to return to a place as you remember it
- Loss of a significant event you thought you'd experience
- Loss of a friendship
- Loss of getting to do something you were looking forward to
- Loss of knowing the rules
- Loss of a place that feels homey
- Loss of independence
- Loss of having someone to invite over when you feel lonely
- Loss of a familiar or comfortable climate
- Loss of closure

Reading and recognizing these can often explain why that obvious loss (like moving) *feels* so hard. It's not just moving that is so hard; it is all of the hidden losses associated with it.

Intense Moments of Fear
These blocks are significant moments or seasons when you felt paralyzed by fear.

These could be:

- Explicit fear-inducing events. These are moments when you felt afraid because something was happening to you: a home invasion, a medical crisis, a car accident, sexual assault, etc.
- Environmental fear. These are fear-inducing experiences that happened around you: a natural disaster, gang violence, unsafe living environments, domestic violence in your home.
- Fear out of concern. These moments involve being terrified for someone else's safety or health.

Each incident that falls in any of these categories would be a block on your Grief Tower.

Seasons of Prolonged Anxiety/Depression
This could be a season when either you or your parent/caregiver experienced prolonged depression or anxiety.

If a parent/caregiver suffered from an unmanaged mental illness and it negatively impacted you, that would be a block on your Grief Tower. An example of this would be a mother who had a season of depression in which she was in bed often and wasn't meeting her children's emotional and/or physical needs well.

Alternatively, this could be a period longer than a couple of weeks when you felt depressed and/or very anxious. If this season was not related to another Grief Tower block, then it is a block of its own. However, if it is directly related to another block, you may decide not to put it as a block on its own.

Family Crises
Examples of crises might include a death in the family, a severe illness in the nuclear family, a traumatic event that happened to a family member, or the divorce of parents. Even if the details of the crisis were kept from you at the time, it's likely you experienced the thick tension, sadness, anger, and other effects within the home that stemmed from that situation or event.

Abuse or Neglect

These may be connected to specific memories, but they might also just be running themes that you remember from your childhood. Perhaps you remember being left alone a lot or never having your emotional needs met by nurturing parents. Maybe you remember being emotionally abused by an angry parent who swore at you and called you names, but you can't remember an exact incident because they all blur together. Perhaps you were raised in a home where addiction was present. These are still "blocks" on your tower, even if it's not possible to put them in chronological order.

Other Difficult Events

This can be thought of as the "catch-all" category. Anything that stands out as a significantly difficult event, memory, situation, or season qualifies as a block on the Grief Tower even if it doesn't fit into the specific categories mentioned. This includes any events or moments that are etched in your brain as feeling very sad, upsetting, or angering.

DOES IT COUNT AS A BLOCK?

When working with individuals on their Grief Tower, I'm often told about an experience and then asked, "Does that count?" If you're asking the question, then the answer is yes. When in doubt, put it on the tower. There is no risk to putting a block on the Grief Tower and taking time to process it; it will only be a positive exercise. I often find that people think it's not significant until they start to process it and realize it is actually a bigger "block" than they realized. So if you are thinking through your blocks and wondering if something "counts," the answer is yes, it does. Put it on the tower.

ACE SCORES

Not all blocks on the Grief Tower carry the same weight. There are some that are much larger and heavier and have the potential for long-term impact. It is important to be aware of these so that we give them the proper care. I refer to these as the "boulders" on your tower. If thinking about these blocks feels distressing or overwhelming, seek out the care of a mental health professional to begin the work of processing them.

These "boulders" can also be categorized as Adverse Childhood Experience (ACE) scores. This concept comes from a study first conducted by Kaiser Permanente from 1995 to 1997. The purpose of the study was to determine how difficult events and experiences that happen to us during our developmental years are tied to our physical, emotional, and mental health as adults. What they found was that when an individual has an ACE score greater than four, they are:

- 2x more likely to develop heart disease or cancer
- 7x times more likely to be alcoholic
- at increased risk of emphysema or chronic bronchitis by nearly 400 percent
- at increased risk of attempted suicide by 1200 percent

People with high ACE scores are more likely to be violent, to have more marriages, more broken bones, more drug prescriptions, more depression, and more autoimmune diseases. People with an ACE score of six or higher are at risk of their lifespan being shortened by 20 years.[5]

This does *not* mean that you are going to experience these

---

5 V. J. Felitti, R. F. Anda, D. Nordenberg, D. F. Williamson, A. M. Spitz, V. Edwards, M. P. Koss, and J. S. Marks. (1998). Relationship of childhood abuse and household dysfunction to many of the leading causes of death in adults: The adverse childhood experiences (ACE) study. *American Journal of Preventive Medicine, 14*, 245–58.

outcomes. ACE studies don't look at individuals; they look at population trends. This means that the population of people who have high ACE scores also tend to have negative adulthood outcomes, but it doesn't predict a specific individual's future because there are resilience factors that come into play that make the individual outcomes vary greatly. At the end of this chapter we'll discuss what that can look like and what you can put into place even now to mitigate the risk of your childhood trauma impacting your health in negative ways in adulthood.

WHAT ARE THE ADVERSE CHILDHOOD EXPERIENCES?

The ten events that constitute ACE scores fall into three main categories: Abuse, Neglect, and Household Dysfunction. They are further categorized as:

Abuse: Physical, emotional, sexual

Neglect: Physical, emotional

Household Dysfunction: Mental illness of a parent, divorce, parental substance abuse, incarcerated member of the household, and parent treated violently

We'll explore each of these ACE factors in greater depth in this chapter.

Your "ACE score" is how many out of these 10 types of trauma happened during your childhood. Most researchers consider a score of more than 4 to be considered a "high" ACE score. Not only are high ACE scores associated with taller Grief Towers, but they are also more likely to contribute to Complex-PTSD because of what those experiences do to a developing brain.

When Adverse Childhood Experiences happen, the child's brain floods with the stress hormones adrenaline and cortisol. This is because their brain has detected a threat, and they need to be ready to respond. Unfortunately when this threat detection happens frequently or for long periods of time, the child's brain marinates in these chemicals, keeping it from developing like it should.

If you notice that you have experiences that fall into these categories, take note of them and consider the extent to which you have processed and healed from them. If you have yet to walk with a professional through processing these, I would encourage you to consider doing so. These boulders should not be picked up alone, so while you may choose to do some of the basic processing that we'll walk through in later chapters, I highly recommend that you don't over-engage these blocks without someone walking alongside you.

ABUSE

Physical
Physical abuse happens anytime someone harms a child on purpose. It includes: hitting with hands or objects, slapping, punching, kicking, or other forms of physical harm.

Emotional
Emotional abuse happens when your emotions are used to manipulate, shame, or harm you.

According to the National Society for the Prevention of Cruelty to Children (NSPCC), emotional abuse can include:

- Humiliating or constantly criticizing a child
- Threatening, shouting at a child, or calling them names
- Making the child feel stupid or using sarcasm to hurt a child
- Blaming and scapegoating

- Making a child perform degrading acts
- Not recognizing a child's natural limitations and pushing them too hard
- Exposing a child to upsetting events such as witnessing violence
- Not allowing a child to have friends
- Persistently ignoring the child
- Being physically or mentally absent
- Manipulating a child
- Never saying anything kind, expressing positive feelings, or congratulating a child on success
- Never showing any emotions when interacting with the child[6]

Sexual

Sexual abuse can be as severe as rape, but it can also be sexual harassment or assault.

Sexual abuse can also include grooming, exposing oneself to a child, obscene digital interaction, or showing pornographic images to a child. Sexual abuse can occur between an adult and a child, but it can also occur between children, also known as Child on Child Sexual Abuse or COCSA. All forms of sexual abuse are considered an ACE score.

NEGLECT

Physical

Physical neglect happens when a parent actively or passively "fails to provide for a child's basic needs, like food, clothing,

---

6 National Society for the Prevention of Cruelty to Children (n.d.). Retrieved September 3, 2023 from https://www.nspcc.org.uk/what-is-child-abuse/types-of-abuse/emotional-abuse/

shelter, education, medical care, or supervision."[7] It also happens when a child is regularly worried that these physical needs won't be met.

Emotional

Emotional neglect can be categorized as passive or active. Active emotional neglect is when a parent consciously decides to ignore the emotions of their child. This is most often due to a parent's mental illness. Passive neglect, on the other hand, is more common. The parent genuinely cares about the child and their needs but simply struggles to meet them.

Passive emotional neglect may have looked like:

- Parents not noticing, responding, or comforting you when you experienced difficult emotions (sadness, anger, nervousness, etc)
- Parents implying or saying that their own challenges are more severe than yours
- Parents seeking comfort from you instead of comforting you
- Parents not listening when you talk, particularly when you're voicing things that feel vulnerable
- Parents being emotionally unavailable to you
- Parents not asking about or validating your preferences, needs, or desires

When this happens to you as a child, you learn:

- That other people's emotions are more important than yours
- That it is worthy to not have preferences, needs, or desires
- Not to speak up for yourself

---

7 South Dakota Department of Social Services. (2020). *Signs of abuse and neglect.* https://dss.sd.gov/childprotection/signs.aspx#:~:text=Physical%20neglect%20 occurs%20when%20a,care%20or%20supervision%20and%20abandonment.

- That your difficult emotions are unwanted, invalid, or unimportant
- To either neglect your own emotional needs or find unhealthy ways to get the attention you're seeking (often through poor behavior)

HOUSEHOLD DYSFUNCTION

Mental Illness of a Parent
The health of a parent directly impacts the health of a child. When a parent experiences a mental illness, it increases the likelihood of all other ACE scores. In TCK Training's research on ACEs in the Third Culture Kid population, we found that 84% of the 1,904 adults surveyed who reported household adult mental illness also had at least one other Adverse Childhood Experience.[8] This means that if the parent is struggling with mental illness, the child is highly likely to experience another ACE score as well.

Incarcerated Household Member
Incarceration disrupts a family and creates an environment where there is potential for increased stress and trauma for the child(ren) in the family. Not only is there often stigma associated with having an incarcerated family member, but anytime someone who lived with a child disappears from the child's life, no matter the reason, it is impactful for the child. Sometimes repeated arrests occur, causing the person to continually come in and out of the child's life. No matter the details of the situation, living in a household impacted by incarceration is impactful to the child and is an ACE score.

---

8 Crossman, T., & Wells, L. (2022, June 7). Caution and hope: The prevalence of adverse childhood experiences in globally mobile third culture kids. https://www.tcktraining.com/research/caution-and-hope-white-paper

Parent Treated Violently

Witnessing a parent being abused either verbally or physically is traumatic for a child. Not only does it challenge the child's sense of safety, they often also feel that they need to do something to protect themselves and the abused parent. It is also common for children to blame themselves for their parent's violent behavior, often resulting in people-pleasing behaviors, self-deprecation, and/or anxious behaviors. Research has shown that "children as young as one year old can manifest heightened distress in response to verbal conflict between parents."[9] Studies have also shown that witnessing violence in the home impacts a child's behavioral, emotional, and developmental health.[10] Living in a home where domestic violence was present is an ACE score and, like the other ACEs, is a significant Grief Tower boulder to be processed.

Divorce

According to the American Psychological Association, 40-50% of first marriages end in divorce. Not only is this a Grief Tower block for the couple experiencing all the grief and loss that comes with divorce, but the impact on the child is also great. The National Library of Medicine says, "Parental divorce/separation is associated with an increased risk for child and adolescent adjustment problems, including academic difficulties (e.g., lower grades and school dropout), disruptive behaviors (e.g., conduct and substance use problems), and depressed mood."[11]

9 Øverlien, C. (2010). Children exposed to domestic violence: Conclusions from the literature and challenges ahead. *Journal of Social Work,* 10(1), 80-97. https://doi.org/10.1177/1468017309350663

10 Devaney, J. (2015). Research review: The impact of domestic violence on children. *Irish Probation Journal,* 12, 79-94.

11 D'Onofrio B., Emery R. (2019). Parental divorce or separation and children's mental health. *World Psychiatry.* (1),100-101. https://doi.org/10.1002/wps.20590.

Substance Abuse

Substance abuse in the home creates an unstable environment for children. Studies show that "the negative impacts of parental Substance Use Disorders (SUDs) on the family include disruption of attachment, rituals, roles, routines, communication, social life, and finances. Families in which there is a parental SUD are characterized by an environment of secrecy, loss, conflict, violence or abuse, emotional chaos, role reversal, and fear."[12] If your parent struggled with substance abuse of any kind, this would be an ACE score and a block on your tower.

WHAT DOES IT MEAN?

ACE scores mean that there were situations in childhood that created an environment in which your brain signaled your adrenal glands to pump out increased and/or prolonged levels of cortisol. Over time, we know that this begins to impact the brain and body, which is why it is correlated with physical, mental, and behavioral challenges in adulthood.

That does *not* mean that you are going to face the physical, mental, and emotional challenges that are associated with Adverse Childhood Experiences. Nor does it mean that there isn't hope for a healthy adulthood.

Instead, they indicate that there are some serious boulders on your Grief Tower that, if left unaddressed, will be given the opportunity to grow and manifest in unhealthy ways. Few things contribute so deeply to the internal narratives we'll explore in this book like ACE scores do. It is important for you to note which of your Grief Tower blocks are also ACE scores so that you can realize their severity and process them effectively.

---

12 Lander L, Howsare J, Byrne M. (2013). The impact of substance use disorders on families and children: from theory to practice. *Social Work Public Health.* 28(3-4):194-205. https://www.doi.org/10.1080/19371918.2013.759005.

WHAT IF IT'S ME?

You may be reading through the ACE factors and realizing that these have been a part of your children's lives. As an adult, you've struggled to be emotionally present for your children, have been divorced, have had substance abuse in your home, or any of the other factors. Reading the list through that lens may have been difficult, alarming, or any number of difficult emotions. Please know that there is hope. That hope may come through a shift in your behavior or environment, and/or it may be through protective factors that you put into place that buffer your children from the impact of high ACEs. While we cannot undo ACEs, we can move forward in ways that bring resilience and healing. Perhaps that will be a wonderful outcome of unstacking your own Grief Tower.

Positive Childhood Experiences (PCEs)

One of the factors that determines how impactful ACEs will be on a child is whether or not they also had Positive Childhood Experiences (PCEs). In the research, if a child had an Adverse Experience but also had the support of PCEs, their rates of mental illness in adulthood dropped by 72%. In short, PCEs are an antidote to the negative impact of ACEs. For those of us who have high ACEs ourselves or know that our children do, this PCEs framework brings so much hope.

The eight Positive Childhood Experiences are:[13]

1. Feeling that feelings can be shared, heard, and validated in the home
2. Belief that the family stands together and prioritizes one another during difficult times

---

13 Bethell, C., Jones, J., Gombojav, N., Linkenbach, J., & Sege, R. (2019). Positive childhood experiences and adult mental and relational health in a statewide sample: Associations across adverse childhood experiences levels. *JAMA Pediatrics, 173*.

3. Feeling safe and protected in the home
4. Feeling supported by a peer group
5. Feeling a sense of belonging in a larger multigenerational group
6. Having family or community traditions to look forward to
7. Feeling a sense of belonging in high school
8. Having two non-parent adults who take a genuine interest in the child

This list of PCEs demonstrates that a young person's needs are met both in the home and in the community.

A study done in 2017 showed that for those who had an ACE score of 3 or more:

- Belonging in a supportive, multigenerational community reduced adulthood physical health challenges by 9%
- Feeling supported by a peer group throughout childhood lowered adulthood depression by 18%
- Belief that the family stands together and prioritizes one another during difficult times lowered adulthood obesity by 14%
- Participating in community traditions correlated with being 10% less likely to smoke cigarettes in adulthood
- Participating in community traditions lowered depression in adulthood by 15%
- A sense of belonging in high school lowered depression in adulthood by 17%[14]

If you had several of the Positive Childhood Experiences in your childhood, that has likely increased your ability to be

---

14 Bethell C, Jones J, Gombojav N, Linkenbach J, Sege R. (2019). Positive childhood experiences and adult mental and relational health in a statewide sample: Associations across adverse childhood experiences levels. *JAMA Pediatrics.* 173(11). https://www.doi.org/10.1001/jamapediatrics.2019.3007

resilient in the face of adversity. It may have even led to you unstacking your Grief Tower along the way.

I remember talking with a young man after I spoke about the Grief Tower at a conference. He came up and said, "Is it possible that mine never stacked too tall because it got unstacked along the way?" He shared how, though he had experienced several traumas in childhood, his parents had been excellent at helping him to process those experiences either in the home or with a counselor. He explained that a lot of the work that I suggested with the Unstacking Method were things he had already done. Amazing! This is my dream for all of the families with children with whom I work, and perhaps that was your experience as well.

But you may be reading that list and realizing that you didn't get those things throughout your childhood, especially at the times you needed them most.

Not having those PCEs that you should have had is a loss worth grieving.

As an adult, I encourage you to put the essence of those PCEs into place in your life. This will not only reduce the symptoms of a tall or crashed Grief Tower, but it will actually increase resilience in the face of new hardships. Adults who have higher ACE scores and lower PCE scores can actually increase their resilience if they create an adulthood where they:

- Have relationships in which feelings can be shared, heard, and validated
- Have friends and/or family (such as a spouse and children) who stand together and prioritize one another during difficult times
- Feel safe and protected in the home
- Feel supported by friends
- Feel a sense of belonging in a larger multigenerational group
- Have family or community traditions to look forward to

One of the most important reasons for unstacking the Grief Tower is because nearly all of these resilience-building factors revolve around relationships. Unprocessed grief often brings unhealthy elements into a relationship, and so the unstacking process of uncovering how your Grief Tower has impacted your present is an important first step toward being in a place where these things can be pursued and maintained long term.

If these aren't in place in your life, I would encourage you to be curious about how your Grief Tower has contributed to that. Then, be vigilant about searching them out as a part of your healing process. Whether or not you had PCEs in childhood, these factors are critical for health and resilience in adulthood and should be intensely pursued.

WHAT IF I CAN'T REMEMBER MY BLOCKS?

Sometimes piecing together events and memories can be challenging, especially the farther you are from your developmental years. Some ideas that can help you to remember events that may be blocks on your timeline are:

- Looking through photos of those years
- Talking about it with a sibling
- Talking through it with your parents
- Looking at yearbooks from schools you attended
- Telling stories of your childhood to a friend
- Jogging your memory with sensory stimuli from that season such as smells, sounds (songs can be helpful), or tastes
- Reading old journals
- Talking with someone who knew you in those seasons
- Looking through saved memorabilia

In some cases, trauma can cause repressed memories. If you think this may be the case, brainstorm and go through the exercises in this book with only the events that you remember. Processing those memories may help you to remember others. If there still seem to be significant gaps in your memory, consider seeking out the help of a trauma therapist. EMDR (Eye Movement Desensitization and Reprocessing) therapy can be an excellent tool for finding and processing repressed memories associated with trauma.

Sometimes simply the act of brainstorming and writing out your timeline can bring up memories. But don't add extra stress to the process by worrying about not remembering. Process what you can remember, and allow more to come to mind naturally or with the help of a therapist.

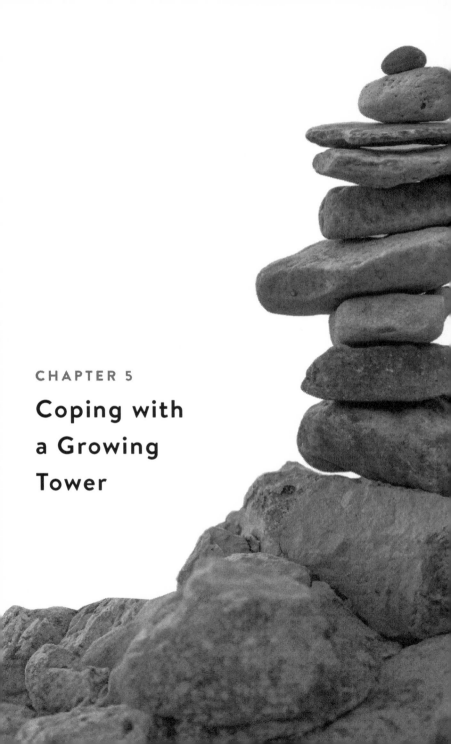

CHAPTER 5

Coping with a Growing Tower

We cope because we don't have a choice – we have to survive. As difficult things happen in our childhood, we learn what works to soothe the pain and get us through. These survival skills, whether they are helpful long term or not, served us at that moment. As our Grief Tower stacks, our coping skills grow in number and intensity. Most of us have a mix of healthy and unhealthy coping skills, and most of us, if we look carefully, can trace the most subconscious ones back to some of our earliest Grief Tower blocks.

For as long as I can remember, my superpower has been being able to nap for hours in any location. During most experiences that I would consider Grief Tower blocks, I can remember saying, "I'm just tired," and I would go off and take a nap. I would exchange any emotion word with "tired" – for example, "I'm not sad, I'm just tired." After my nap, I would get up and distract myself.

As a child, I remember learning that I could get lost in another world by reading books, especially a series because I could live in that world with those characters for longer. This rhythm seemed to be the only way to avoid the surrounding chaos and difficult emotions. When I was asleep, I didn't have to think, and when I woke up, distracting myself kept me from feeling emotion.

As a wife, mom, and business owner, my pattern shifted from fiction reading to a fast-paced hustle in emotionally difficult times. Take a nap, wake up and be ridiculously productive, don't stop until bedtime, repeat. No space for feeling. Years ago I shared with a counselor that I was struggling with anxiety, and she asked, "So what do you do when you start to feel that way?" I said, "I sleep, or I become wildly productive." Those were my go-to coping skills.

I've learned over the years to recognize this tendency and notice when I begin to turn to sleep and busyness as coping mechanisms. I know that when slowing down begins to feel uncomfortable, there is something underlying that I need to process.

My go-to coping skills are not new; they were developed at a young age as a direct response to my Grief Tower.

Some of the most common unhealthy coping skills are:

Numbing – "turning off" emotion so you don't feel anything, using substances to numb, sleeping, overeating, reading or watching television in order to be in a world other than your own.

Distraction – technology, video games, busyness, new relationships (romantic or otherwise), taking on other people's problems.

Isolation – avoiding people (especially those who know you best) so you don't have to talk about what's going on, being antisocial, not making new friends in a new place.

Over-positivity – ignoring the grief by saying, "It'll be ok!" or not processing because "It got better," telling jokes/being funny when things are hard, not allowing yourself to "go there" when experiencing a difficult emotion, using spirituality by thinking/saying, "But God used it for good." These may all be true statements, but they shouldn't be used as a reason to avoid processing.

Negative Self-Talk – degrading yourself for having emotions or for thinking that something is hard, saying, "I'm so weak!" "Get it together!" or "I'm just an idiot and can't do anything well." Thinking, "If I just...(were smarter, tried harder, weren't so emotional, etc.)."

Blaming – blaming everything on the people, location, or circumstances that caused the grief. Acknowledging that it was difficult is not the same as avoiding the grief through the coping skill of blame.

Romanticizing – only acknowledging the positive parts of your past, feeling shame around admitting that there were hard parts as well.

There are, of course, also healthy coping skills that may have been developed during our developmental years or learned since. A while back, I began to go to a CrossFit gym regularly. If you would have told me three years ago that I'd be typing that line, I would have laughed at you. I've always been active, but I hadn't ever done formal workouts – especially those that involve lifting heavy barbells. But I've discovered that not only do I love it, it also helps significantly with anxiety and creating healthy space for emotion. In hard seasons, it has been an incredibly helpful coping skill. I can let out any pent-up, difficult emotions by running faster or lifting heavier.

But I still have to intentionally use this newfound coping skill: I have to decide to drive myself to the gym instead of slipping back into my old habits of sleeping and distracting, which often sound better than a workout in the moment. Often the healthy coping skills we use are ones we've had to learn in adulthood, and if we're not careful, we'll slip right back into the ones that were formed when our Grief Tower first began to stack.

It is important to recognize that even healthy coping skills can become unhealthy if used for unhealthy coping purposes. For example, I still occasionally enjoy a good power nap, and I still love to read, but I keep a pulse on when it shifts from an enjoyable way to recharge to a way to avoid feeling emotions and to escape from my reality (distracting and/or numbing). If going to the gym became a way to distract from difficult emotions instead of a space to reconnect with my body or regulate emotion, then it wouldn't be serving its purpose as a healthy coping skill.

Healthy coping should be a catalyst for processing. An experience with my daughter illustrates this concept well.

We were getting ready to head to a family birthday party

when my then six-year-old told me that she didn't want to go because there would be a lot of people there whom she didn't know, and that made her feel anxious. I said, "That makes sense! I get anxious sometimes when I'm in a room full of people I don't know. If you need a break when we're there to take some deep breaths and get away from the crowd for a minute, just come get me and tell me you need a break, and we'll find a quiet place to go."

About twenty minutes into the party, she came to tell me she needed a break. I took her hand, and we went into a bedroom. "This is better," she said. "Now the two of us can just play in here until the party's over." "Nope," I said. "Remember, we're taking a break *so that* you're ready to go back in."

That is the difference between using a coping skill as a way to regulate yourself so you can get back to processing and using it to keep you from ever processing.

How long you need to cope to be ready to "go back in" depends on the situation. In seasons of crisis, it may be necessary to just cope and survive until the crisis has passed. If processing an early-life Grief Tower block causes an intense reaction, it may be that you need to cope until you can get an appointment with a mental health professional. Or it may be that you simply need to put this book down and switch to a fiction novel for the evening so you can escape momentarily before diving back in.

Some healthy coping skills could be reading, cooking, exercising, journaling, playing an instrument, walking, traveling, writing poetry, making art, spending time with friends, or dancing. Again, it isn't about the action; it's about the purpose. Are you using it to recharge, be introspective, rest, get to a mental space where you can lean into your emotions? Or are you using it to escape and avoid experiencing, feeling, and processing difficult things?

Healthy coping is a temporary escape, not a long-term solution.

Exercise #1: What *unhealthy* coping skills have you used in the past?

Exercise #2: What *healthy* coping skills could replace the *unhealthy* ones you listed above if you are tempted to turn to those?

Exercise #3: Are there people in your life who encourage your *healthy* coping skills and with whom you can spend more time as you work through unstacking? Are there people who encourage *unhealthy* coping skills with whom you should limit time or be cautious around?

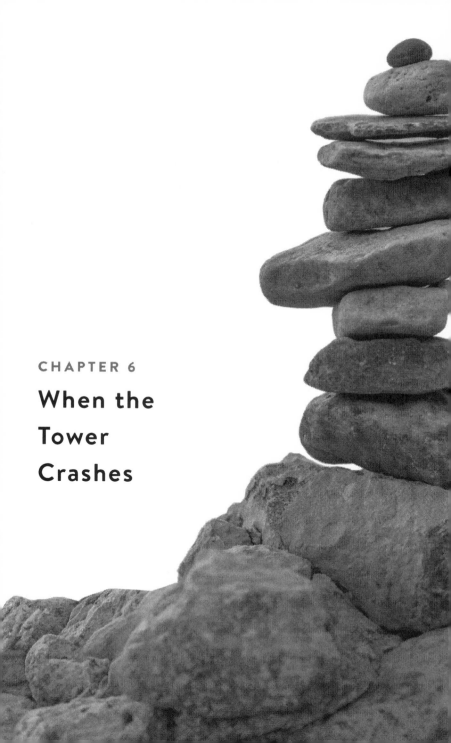

CHAPTER 6

When the Tower Crashes

I f you've ever stacked blocks, you know that no matter how hard you try to get your tower taller than the last time, eventually the tower comes tumbling down.

One of the most significant reasons why we need to unstack our Grief Tower is because of what it does to our body when it's not unstacked. When hard things happen in our life and we never process them, our bodies respond. We were not designed to walk through life shouldering a heavy barbell of past grief. When we do, eventually we notice that something isn't working.

MY TOWER

Up until I was twelve years old, I lived a pretty cushy life. We had a beautiful house with a pool in California (and an epic zipline that allowed us to fly over and drop into the pool). I had great friends and loving parents. I'd imagine that my Grief Tower up until that point had maybe four blocks on it – certainly not many.

Just before I turned thirteen, my parents announced to my younger brother and me that we would be moving to Africa. At that moment we took on a new life as a missionary family. It was in direct correlation to our new life as a missionary family that my Grief Tower stacked tall and fast. Between the stress that spun our home life into chaos to the traumatic experiences that never seemed to stop, it was a perfect storm for growing grief with little support to process it all well.

This is how my tower stacked:

> **Block #1:** At 13 years old we moved from California, U.S.A., to Tanzania, East Africa, saying goodbyes to the friends, family, places, and potential memories we were giving up with those people in that place.

Block #2: During our first week in Tanzania, I watched from a taxi window as a thief was dragged into an angry crowd, a gasoline-soaked tire was thrown over him, and both were lit on fire. He was burned to death to pay for his crime as I looked on, unsure whether to stare or squeeze my eyes shut.

Block #3: I started attending an international school, but unlike many international school contexts, I was the first "new kid" to enter my class in several years. The others had been together since preschool. I was also the only American. While my peers weren't blatantly unkind to me, I felt incredibly out of place and alone. Most days that year I ate lunch by myself behind the school.

Block #4: We went back to the U.S. for a summer, and I realized how much I had been changed by Africa. I realized that although I still felt like a foreigner in Africa, I also felt like I didn't fit back in America either. I felt stupid when I didn't understand the references girls my age made, and I was laughed at for my naivete. I grieved the fact that I didn't fit in completely in either place. I didn't know if I ever would.

Block #5: Back in Africa, we took a boy named Samuel into our home who was dying of HIV/AIDS. He was my age and had been kicked out of his home because of the diagnosis. After living with us for months, eating flying termites out of the air because he thought it was funny to watch me gag, running around the house with my brother and me, and learning how to do the "worm" dance on our green-tile living room floor, he died a horrible death in a dingy African hospital.

Block #6: In true Maasai tribe style, the grieving over his death involved screaming and wailing throughout the village for days. The memory of that sound still gives me chills.

Block #7: My two closest friends moved away within two weeks of each other. I felt incredibly alone.

Block #8: Only a couple of weeks later, a neighbor came to our door and told me that a Tanzanian friend of mine had died in her sleep. I couldn't believe it and ran to her house, only to discover that he was telling the truth. Her father told me she had lain down to take a nap and had never woken up. More wailing rang out through the neighborhood.

Block #9: The next month, a tumultuous election took place in Kenya. Expatriate refugees descended on us, coming to stay until things settled down. Around that time, we were told we needed to move back to the U.S. immediately. We left with only a few days' notice, leaving our life in Africa without the closure of goodbyes.

Block #10 (and probably more): I started my sophomore year at a public high school in California. For me, this was the toughest transition by far as I struggled to make friends and quietly carried the unprocessed grief of our years in Africa. Thinking each month that we were going back to Tanzania the next, we lived in temporary housing, eventually totaling 18 houses that year.

Block #11: We moved back to Africa, to a new city that was ten hours from the first. I said goodbye once again to the friends that I'd finally made back in the U.S.

Block #12: I went straight from Africa to Indiana to start university. I was excited and enthusiastic, but another big change on top of all of the previous years of change and trauma didn't set me up for success.

Even as I write this, I can remember feeling the intensity and angst increase as the hard things piled up. It's no wonder those years felt so hard.

My Grief Tower crashed during my sophomore year of university. I had not processed any of what had happened during the years when my tower was stacking. When I did let myself think about the hard things, I felt numb, as if those memories were emotionally off limits. That year, I moved into an apartment by myself, worked an early morning shift at a coffee shop, took classes in the afternoon, worked the dinner shift as a server, and spent the weekends working for a church as the music director. This crazy schedule was the only feasible way that I could find to pay my way through college, and honestly, I didn't mind it. I liked my independent, fast-paced life.

That year, I began having horrible nightmares. They often took place in Africa, and I always woke up yelling, sweaty, and panting. Around the same time, I discovered an unexplained, quarter-sized bald spot on my head. I was battling never-ending cold sores on my lips and had constant stomach aches. I had no idea these were symptoms of a crashed Grief Tower. I went to the doctor and was told that all my bloodwork looked normal; that I should take vitamins and try changing my diet. I cut out dairy and trudged on.

At some point in all of that I got engaged, so wedding planning got thrown into the mix.

After my Grief Tower crashed, life kept going. Our first year of marriage included an ectopic pregnancy. We thought I was 10 weeks pregnant and by that point had spent months talking about names and dreams for our baby. On Mother's Day weekend we discovered that the egg was never in the right place. I cried for a moment, pulled myself up, and said I was fine.

Three months later, we moved across the country from

Indiana to Oregon, starting a life from scratch. I began a job at a law firm where roll was taken at 8 am every morning. If you were late, you were fired on the spot. Each morning involved a spiel about how replaceable we all were. Once I made a typo on a form, and a lady charged down from the second floor to berate me in front of the entire staff, yelling, "How are you this stupid!?" and shouting that I wouldn't amount to anything in life.

My last week working at that law firm (and just a couple of days after my birthday), I experienced labor pains for the first time as I contracted in the dark staff bathroom and pushed out a teeny tiny 8-week-old baby. I'd had another miscarriage. I vividly remember trying to decide what to do with the tiny little almost-body. Flushing it seemed so wrong, but also, what was I supposed to do with it? I shook and sobbed in every kind of pain until I could pull myself together, exit back out into the office, and tell my boss I needed a sick day.

That week I told my husband that I needed to go to counseling. I wasn't doing well, and I knew I hadn't been since sophomore year of college. My body was carrying every hard thing that had happened.

My wonderful therapist specialized in trauma, and as I unpacked my life in Africa and my life since then, she explained how trauma resides in the body, described what that looks like, and gave words to everything I had experienced up to that point. After finding language for what I had been experiencing – Complex-PTSD – I began a long healing journey of finally looking back so that I could move forward into a healthier future.

I learned the hard way that our bodies were not designed to carry the weight of hardship and trauma without response. We can ignore it. We can be busy and tough and optimistic. But our body doesn't let us off the hook.

BUT IS IT "*TRAUMA*"?

Like I mentioned in Chapter 4, the words we use to label our Grief Tower blocks may vary. However, sometimes the use of the word "trauma" is helpful, especially when we're looking into the research around the effect that the hard things that have happened to us, especially in our developmental years, have on our brain. Often the skepticism is rooted in the fact that the word "trauma" has become a Gen Z buzzword that can be overused – "I took a sip of my latte, and it was whole milk instead of the oat milk I'd ordered. It was so traumatic!"

However, there *is* a time and place for that word, and it's not only for the most horrific events and experiences that we can conjure up in our imagination. According to the Centre for Addiction and Mental Health, "Trauma is a term used to describe the challenging emotional consequences that living through a distressing event can have for an individual. Traumatic events can be difficult to define because the same event may be more traumatic for some people than for others."[15]

In the example with the oat milk, perhaps the person drinking the latte was deathly allergic to dairy and had to be hospitalized because of the sip of the allergen. For them, a mixup of milk may have genuinely been traumatic. But for someone who doesn't have a dairy allergy and is just annoyed that the barista got their order wrong, the original sentence would be an overuse of the word. What is traumatic for you may not be traumatic for someone else, but that doesn't mean the word isn't important or that the event itself doesn't deserve to be processed.

Sometimes a differentiation is made between big "T" traumas and small "t" traumas. Big "T" traumas are defined

---

15 Centre for Addiction and Mental Health. (n.d.). *Trauma.* Retrieved September 5, 2023 from https://www.camh.ca/en/health-info/mental-illness-and-addiction-index/trauma

as "extraordinary and significant events that leave the individual feeling powerless and possessing little control in their environment. Such events could take the form of a natural disaster, terrorist attack, sexual assault, combat, a car or plane accident, etc." Small "t" traumas, on the other hand, "are events that exceed our capacity to cope and cause a disruption in emotional functioning."[16]

Many times, the blocks on our Grief Tower are what would be considered small "t" traumas. For some of us, there may also be some big "T" traumas. Either way, they are considered blocks on our Grief Tower because they were difficult events that impacted our present.

WHAT TRAUMA DOES TO OUR BODY

If we go through an intense trauma (those big "T" trauma experiences), Post-Traumatic Stress Disorder (PTSD) may be the response, but trauma is often more complex and covert than that. It's not one big thing that happened; it's a continuous stream of those smaller, seemingly insignificant losses or long-ago small "t" traumas that stack up. As they stack, our brain becomes increasingly sensitive to what it believes to be threats. Our fight-or-flight response gets out of whack, and the rhythm of having our brain flooded with stress hormones too often or for too long begins to take its toll.

The book *The Body Keeps the Score* by Bessel van der Kolk looks extensively at this phenomenon. Van der Kolk says, "We have learned that trauma is not just an event that took place sometime in the past; it is also the imprint left by that experience on mind, brain, and body. This imprint has ongoing

---

16 Barbash, Elyssa. (2017). Different types of trauma: Small 't' versus large 'T' An accumulation of smaller or less pronounced events can still be traumatic. *Psychology Today.*

consequences for how the human organism manages to survive the present."[17]

Whether you would label the blocks on your Grief Tower "trauma" or not, they still impact your present and may contribute to the ongoing consequences van der Kolk was referring to. These ongoing consequences often show up in our body when difficult things accumulate without time and space to grieve and process them. When that happens, the Grief Tower continues to grow taller and eventually crashes.

Some common symptoms of a crashed Grief Tower (or accumulated trauma) are:

- Stomach issues
- Increased anxiety
- Hair loss
- Jumpiness/feeling on edge
- Autoimmune disorders
- Fibromyalgia or other chronic pain
- Canker sores or cold sores
- Racing heart or heart palpitations
- Skin issues such as rashes or itching
- Nightmares
- Other physical or mental health challenges that seem to have no explanation

The symptoms above may be entirely medical, so it's important to consult with your doctor if you're experiencing these, but it is also possible that you are experiencing the symptoms of a crashed Grief Tower.

Sometimes, a crashed Grief Tower is diagnosed as Complex-PTSD, as was the case for me. The symptoms often look very similar to PTSD, but for Complex-PTSD there's no

---

17 Bessel Van Der Kolk, M.D. (2014). *The body keeps the score: Brain, mind, and body in the healing of trauma.* Penguin Books. 21.

specific event that is the cause. Intead, it's many smaller events that cause the brain to habitually overreact. Complex-PTSD is a physical response to prolonged or repeated trauma over a long period of time.[18] The symptoms of complex trauma are broad and are often a mystery to doctors and psychologists alike. Psychologist Dr. Glenn Doyal says, "The 'complex' in complex trauma isn't just about its origin. It's also about how that trauma shows up in our bodies, lives and relationships."[19]

Not everyone who has a tall Grief Tower will experience Complex-PTSD, but if there has been a continuous stream of small or big trauma throughout your life, it may be that Complex-PTSD explains some symptoms and challenges you've been having.

Whether or not your crashed tower leads to a diagnosis, you have two choices:

1. Process the blocks to allow your brain and body to release them and heal.
2. Cope with the crash and remain in survival mode.

When we process the blocks, we create space to investigate the hard thing that happened – allowing ourselves to name and feel the emotions that came with that experience, discover the way that experience shaped us, and find ways that we can use that experience to propel us going forward. This book will teach you how to go through that process.

However, coping may be necessary in the short term or along the way, as we discussed in the previous chapter.

In the short term, it may be necessary to cope with your crashed tower in order to survive and take care of your current

---

18 Keeley, G.M. Reed, M.C. Roberts, S.C. Evans, R. Robles, C. Matsumoto, A. Maercker. (2016). Disorders specifically associated with stress: a case-controlled field study for ICD-11 mental and behavioural disorders. Int. J. Clin. Health Psychol. 16(2). 109-127. https://doi.org/10.1016/j.ijchp.2015.09.002

19 Doyle, Glenn Patrick. [@drdoyalsays]

responsibilities. As you go through this unstacking process, you may find you need to set this book down and pull out a coping skill to re-regulate yourself. However, coping should be a means to get you to a time and space where you have the capacity to begin or resume processing.

In the midst of a crisis, processing is not helpful and can actually be harmful. Psychological First Aid trainers teach that during a crisis, practitioners need to prioritize ongoing safety and provide physical and emotional comfort.

> *If you are currently in crisis, please do not continue through this book. Please seek a trained therapist for support or call the United States Crisis Hotline (988).*

BUILDING ON THE RUBBLE

If you only cope with your crashed tower and never process, the hard things that continue to come in life will only be stacking on top of the rubble. One by one they'll grow taller and taller until that tower is ready to crash. Unfortunately there's no loophole to unstacking. If you don't process your Grief Tower, it will eventually come tumbling down. When it does, you can repeat that same process, getting further and further into unhealthy territory, or you can pick up the blocks and start unstacking.

If you're reading this and think that your Grief Tower has already crashed (or perhaps has multiple times), you're carrying too much rubble. Your crashed tower is impacting you in ways that you probably don't even realize. The physical symptoms are just manifestations of what's going on internally, and it's the internal part that needs to be dealt with before the physical can heal.

If you haven't experienced a Grief Tower crash, wonderful! I am a huge advocate for preventive healing. Preventive healing means doing the work to process how your past has impacted you so that you can heal from the things you didn't know were affecting you so deeply.

However you're coming into this journey, you're in the right place. We've all got stuff to unstack, and it's time to take that step.

> **Exercise #1:** Do you think you have experienced a crashed Grief Tower? If so, can you pinpoint when and what led up to it? Have you processed the blocks that came before the crash, or have you been building on the rubble?

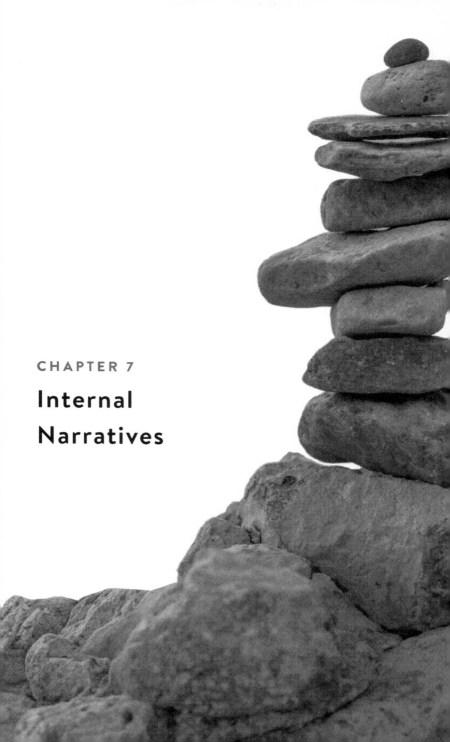

CHAPTER 7

Internal
Narratives

"One of the new things people began to find out in the last century was that thoughts – just mere thoughts – are as powerful as electric batteries – as good for one as sunlight is, or as bad for one as poison."

—Frances Hodgson Burnett in *The Secret Garden*

We all have lines we tell ourselves – statements that we believe to be deeply true because our life experience tells us so. If you listen to people through the lens of this Grief Tower concept, you'll hear narratives coming out all over the place. Most books and movies feature a main character who is battling a harmful internal narrative, and the happy ending is a disproving of that narrative.

Think about the Disney Classic, *Beauty and the Beast*. The Beast had come to believe that he was unlovable. This "I'm unlovable" narrative drove him to sadness and anger, creating a castle filled with creatures who were terrified of his temper. As Belle began to befriend the Beast, he began to see that his narrative might actually be incorrect. He might not be unlovable after all.

Sometimes, writers will even show you how that narrative began by cutting to a scene of the character's childhood to show the trauma, hurt, or experience that caused the child to develop the narrative that they're living by in the present day.

One evening I was reading *The Secret Garden* with my two girls. As Mary, the main character, is sailing from India to England to live with her uncle, the story tells us that her uncle, Mr. Craven, is a mean man. Audrey, my youngest, asked, "Mom, why is he mean?" and Clara, my oldest, answered, "Something really sad probably happened to him." *(Apparently this is what happens when you have a grief specialist for a mother.)* We quickly found out that she was correct. Mr. Craven's wife had fallen off a swing when she was pregnant, killing her and harming the baby.

If you look for the Grief Tower concept – that hard things in our past create narratives that we live out in our present – you'll find it in almost any story. Unstacking our Grief Tower starts with figuring out what our blocks have caused us to believe so that we can decide whether that belief is helpful and will serve us going forward, or whether it is harmful and will lead us in unhealthy directions.

NARRATIVES

We create narratives to explain an event and/or our response to it. Sometimes this comes from our own internal processing of the situation, while other times it comes from someone speaking it over us.

I was working with a young man who was sharing about his current struggles in university. He kept talking about his younger brother, a freshman, and he would continuously mention ways he was going above and beyond to support his brother, including feeling responsible for his brother's grades and social life. I said, "It sounds like you've taken on a lot of responsibility for your brother since he came to school." He said, "Well, yeah, I have to!"

As we dug into his Grief Tower Timeline, I learned that his father had a long battle with cancer starting when he, the son, was eleven years old. For a long period of time, his father was undergoing treatment that made him weak and unable to be active in his boys' lives. He told his son, "I need you to be the man of the house and take care of your mom and younger brother."

Though his father beat the cancer, that narrative held strong. Each time his father left on a business trip, this son acted out the role of being the "man of the house" and taking care of everyone else.

For him to not continue in this role when his brother joined him at university felt absurd. After all, that was his role, and he'd played it well since he was eleven years old.

The hard things that happen in our life shape how we view ourselves, relationships, the world, and God. In the following chapters, we'll dive into each of those areas and spend time looking at how your Grief Tower wrote internal narratives into your life. Then you'll have the opportunity to discern whether those narratives will continue to be helpful if you live by them going forward.

Unhealthy or unhelpful narratives are incredibly covertly destructive. We often don't know that they're there, so they sneakily wreak havoc on our identity and relationships, like a disease brewing undetected under the surface. But as with a disease, eventually the symptoms will start to creep up. Often the first symptoms are emotions like resentment, anxiety, bitterness, anger, and hatred. But then our physical body also starts to respond through exhaustion, hyperawareness, numbness, chronic pain, headaches, and/or stomach issues like we explored in the previous chapter.

The reason this happens is because narratives are most often connected to difficult events that happened in our developmental years. This means that they were often created in a moment when our brain decided that we needed that belief in order to survive. For example, someone who suffered abuse as a child may have subconsciously decided, "The world isn't safe," and they've moved forward in life with their body and brain believing and responding to people and situations from that lens. It started out as a survival response, which is why it's so deeply ingrained in the parts of the brain responsible for keeping us alive.

And this is why these internal narratives have such a strong hold on us. Not only do we *think* that they are true, but everything in our brain and body has been wired to believe and respond as if living them out is the only way to stay alive.

These narratives tend to be so deep in our wiring and to impact so much of our life because we've never named them and decided cognitively whether they were helpful to us. We've let them run the show on the emotional side of our brain but never brought our logical brain online to actually evaluate whether that was a good idea or not.

Our narratives also impact those around us, particularly if those around us are children who are learning how the world works and developing their own set of internal narratives. Even if you don't intend it, the narratives you live by will likely be picked up by the developing brains around you and thus, passed onto the next generation. Sometimes the best way to begin to decipher if a narrative is good and healthy is by asking ourselves if this is something we'd want our child or grandchild to live by in their life.

The first step to rewiring our internal narratives is to cognitively identify what they are and then develop combating narratives to replace the unhealthy ones. It isn't until we take those steps that we can bring the emotional side back into the conversation to emotionally process the experience that led to the unhealthy narrative. It is through the process of doing these things that the block on our tower can get unstacked.

COMBATING NARRATIVES

Creating combating narratives is one of the most important and impactful components of unstacking your Grief Tower. These combating narratives are the things that you say to yourself to counteract what you have identified as harmful or unhelpful internal narratives. A unique (and powerful) aspect of the Grief Tower method is that these narratives aren't rote truth or nice sentiments that could be true for everyone. Instead, they are deeply personal because they were mined out of the difficult things that have happened in your life. Your set of combating narratives will likely not match anyone else's because they are tied to your unique story.

The purpose of combating narratives is to combat the half truths of the harmful narratives by speaking words that counteract the logic of the harmful narratives. If we just focused on not thinking about the harmful narratives but didn't have anything to replace them with, our attempt would be unproductive at best and more than likely would be so disheartening that it would be easy to give up trying. Remember that your harmful narratives have been so deeply dug into your being that they're not going to be undone easily, and certainly not by just focusing on not thinking about or acting on them. You'll never win that battle.

Author and speaker Bob Goff talks about a wood-fired hot tub at his cabin in Canada. He shares that when it's time to heat it for the season, the tub is always filled with leaves and pine needles. If you were to attempt to clean it by picking the leaves and pine needles out of the water, it would take an eternity and you'd be so frustrated you'd never finish. Instead, the solution for getting the foliage out of the hot tub is filling it with more water and letting it overflow. The debris rises to the top and eventually spills out as the clean water takes over.[20]

Focusing on the harmful or unhelpful narratives is like trying to pick the leaves out of the hot tub one by one. Significantly more effective is focusing on the combating narratives, or truth statements, and allowing those to fill your mind and heart until slowly, slowly, they become your predominant narratives.

Combating narratives directly counteract a single harmful narrative. The tricky thing is that you've believed your unhelpful narratives for so long that they seem true. You may still look at your list of narratives and have a difficult time believing that those aren't accurate because the evidence that you've collected through your life seems to validate those beliefs. Again, it's important to consider how those narratives will impact you if they continue to direct your thoughts, choices, and behaviors. Perhaps they already have. If those narratives don't lead to a place that you want to go, then they need to

20 Goff, Bob. (Host). *Ann Voskamp.* [Audio podcast]. Dream Big Podcast.

be combatted *even if you're not yet convinced they aren't true.*

Because of the challenge of disbelieving our unhelpful narratives, it can be helpful to remove your own experiences and emotions from the equation as you begin to construct combating narratives. One helpful method is to think about what you would say to a friend struggling with your internal narratives. We typically have more optimism and hope for our friends' situations than we do for our own.

So while you may think, "I can't trust anyone," and you have a difficult time finding a narrative to combat that belief in a way that feels true to you, if you had a friend say, "I'm really struggling to believe I can trust anyone," what would you say to them? Perhaps something like, "You can't trust a lot of people, but there are some you can." Or, "I'm someone you can trust." Simply by believing yourself trustworthy, you're poking holes in the narrative, "I can't trust anyone." Surely you're not the only person on the planet who is worthy of trust. As you look through your narratives, consider your honest response if a friend were to come to you struggling with that narrative.

Another helpful method is to bring safe, trustworthy people into the conversation who can bring insight as you hunt for combating narratives. We love to facilitate Unstacking Groups because it creates the perfect environment for this. Not everyone's narratives are the same, so there are likely people who can help you develop combating narratives because their struggle is different from yours, and thus, their perspective on your harmful narratives can provide combating words.

For example, if you share, "I'm really struggling with the belief that it's my job to keep everyone happy," you may have a friend who says, "That's a lot of pressure to put on yourself, and it doesn't sound like that's healthy for you or anyone else. You can certainly care well for people without being responsible for their emotions." In this way we can invite our friends to help us find combating narratives – and write a different story for ourselves. If you don't have people in your life to play this role, seeking out a counselor to help you pinpoint internal narratives and wordsmith combating narratives may be a good next step.

As you begin to develop combating narratives throughout the following chapters, here are a few things to keep in mind.

First, combating narratives should not use all-or-nothing language or be the direct opposite of your harmful narrative. Harmful narratives are rarely 100% incorrect – after all, you have a whole lifetime of evidence proving their veracity. Because of that, an opposite narrative would not only be entirely unbelievable, it also wouldn't be true and, thus, would probably be just as harmful. For example, if your unhelpful narrative is, "I can't trust anyone," the combating narrative shouldn't be, "I can trust everyone." Instead it could be, "Some people are trustworthy." That narrative invites you to believe that finding someone trustworthy is possible while also providing the caution that not everyone is, and thus, you still have to be mindful about whom you trust.

Second, combating narratives should welcome feelings such as hope, peace, comfort, contentment, and joy. That does not mean that they won't feel uncomfortable. When you're unlearning something that has felt foundational to your life, it's going to feel incredibly uncomfortable. But combating narratives should breed some sense of hope. This is why the suggestion of considering what you'd tell a friend is helpful. If a friend is struggling, you're likely going to want to tell them something that inspires hope, peace, comfort, contentment, or joy. Your combating narratives should do that for you.

Finally, many of the people with whom I have worked come from a Christian background and like to use Biblical scripture as their combating narratives. There can be great truth narratives that come from scripture that could be helpful, and if you discover some that speak directly to your narrative, then by all means, use those. However, over the years I've observed a tendency to use a very broad spiritual narrative to encompass several unhelpful narratives in a general manner. For example, if the narratives are, "I'm too sensitive," "The world is unsafe," or "I have to be perfect," then using the phrase "God loves me" as your combating narrative for all of those isn't likely to be effective. One reason is that our combating narratives need to be as specific as our harmful narratives are.

The other reason is that the broad use of scripture like that tends to create a "so it doesn't matter" statement. Instead of "I'm too sensitive" being combatted with "God created emotions, and feeling and expressing them can be good and healthy," it turns into "I'm too sensitive, but God loves me, so it doesn't matter." With this method, you never actually combat the narrative and provide opportunity to heal from it; you just dismiss and cover it up. Again, scripture can be a great source of combating narratives, but it needs to be specific. For example, if the unhelpful narrative is, "I can't be weak," a great scriptural combating narrative could be, "God's grace is sufficient for me, and God shows up in my weakness" (from 2 Corinthians 12:9).

Here are some examples of harmful narratives and potential combating narratives. There may be some below that resonate with you, some that you can tweak, and some that you'll need to invent to combat your unique unhelpful narratives.

"My feelings don't matter." → "There's space for my emotions."

"I have to take care of everyone." → "Taking on responsibility for everyone isn't helpful for me or them."

"I have to be perfect." → "Growth can't happen without making mistakes."

"I have to give 100% to everything I do." → "I need to allow some areas of life to receive less than my best effort, so that the important ones can receive my best."

"I take up too much space." → "It's healthy to bring my strength and confidence to a space and to create space for others to do the same."

NOTICING A NARRATIVE

Sometimes you find your narratives by looking at the blocks, and other times you find the narrative first and then investigate whether or not there's a block connected to it. This is something that I've found happens even after you've done the work of unstacking. With this Grief Tower lens, you begin to notice patterns more easily and then move with curiosity toward uncovering why that pattern is there, what grief block it's connected to, and how you might combat it.

At my company TCK Training, the overarching team value that sums up the list of values we uphold in the workplace is, "We practice what we preach." If we're a company that educates and creates trainings and resources on emotional health, grief processing, and being an emotionally safe space, then we had better be doing that for each other as well.

This means that in our casual work conversations, we respond in emotionally safe ways. For example, if an intern presents their workload and says they feel a bit overwhelmed, you can pretty much guarantee that their supervisor will say something like, "That does sound like a lot! It totally makes sense that you would feel overwhelmed. What would help make your workload more manageable?" We've had several interns comment on how they've learned in their time with us that there is almost always a "TCK Training response."

But for others of us, especially those of us who have worked together for a long time, the conversations sometimes go much deeper than that. One of us might send a message that says, "I think I have something I need to verbally process. Do you have the capacity for that today?"

I reached out with a similar ask not too long ago. When my coworker said, "Yes, absolutely," I walked into her virtual office (yes, we have virtual offices – with desks, decor, pictures of our families on the wall, and even a bottle of virtual champagne for when we need to celebrate), and we began to chat.

I said, "I think there's an internal narrative that I just can't put my finger on, but I'm noticing it coming out. I need help brainstorming."

I went on to explain a scenario that seemed to keep repeating with my husband, Aaron.

Aaron would be stressed and would share that stress with me. I would validate and encourage. But then, I would take it a step further and begin to offload all of the things that I could from him onto me. "You know what, I'll take the car to the shop and run to the store for you. I'll even take the kids with me so you can have the house to yourself. Do you want to go to the gym tonight? I'll skip so that you can have that time to recharge."

It wouldn't always be as obvious as that, but I was noticing that this theme kept arising. He would be stressed, and I would add to my plate. I started to wonder why I was responding that way. After all, I was stressed too. I also had a huge to-do list, and getting to the gym was something I'd been looking forward to all day.

My coworker listened and said, "I wonder if you feel like you can't be okay unless he's okay?"

In a way she was right, but I thought I had already dealt with that. I knew that I wasn't responsible for the emotions of others and had spent years in counseling learning how to act on that knowledge. In the past my actions would have been laced with codependency – "I can't be okay unless you're okay, so I need to do whatever it takes to make sure you're okay." Counseling and years of practice had helped me separate my well-being from other people's emotions. Yet, here I was, feeling that same narrative slipping back in, though with a slightly different twist.

As we talked, I realized it was more about, "If there's something I *could* do to help, why wouldn't I?" That seemed like the kind, loving thing to do. And sometimes, it absolutely is! But this narrative combined with another that I'm eternally combating – "I can always take on more" – meant that I wasn't putting limits around what I could and should be offering to take on. Consistently responding to his stress or difficult emotions (and everyone else's) in this way wasn't going to lead to health for either of us.

"What might a good combating narrative be that would remind you that you don't have to take everything on yourself?" my coworker asked.

"I don't need to be the savior?"

No, not quite...

"Carrying everything on my own isn't a healthy solution?"

Maybe, but still not quite...

"It's okay to let people struggle even when there's something I could do to help?"

Ooooh, yeah...that's it.

You know you've hit the deep combating narrative when it feels a bit like a punch in the gut. It feels slightly unbelievable, but also very accurate. It feels incredibly uncomfortable and like you're going to need some convincing that it's actually true.

When I work with clients to unstack their Grief Tower, we brainstorm potential combating narratives until they have that feeling. Usually the response when we've hit it is something like, "Ouch, yep. That's it."

As you're working on finding your internal narratives and combating narratives, or helping others to find theirs, pay attention to the emotions that arise. Both the deeply held internal narrative and the combating narrative will elicit some sort of emotional response. That's because your body knows that narrative, and your body isn't quite ready to let the harmful one go and believe that the combating narrative really is helpful and true.

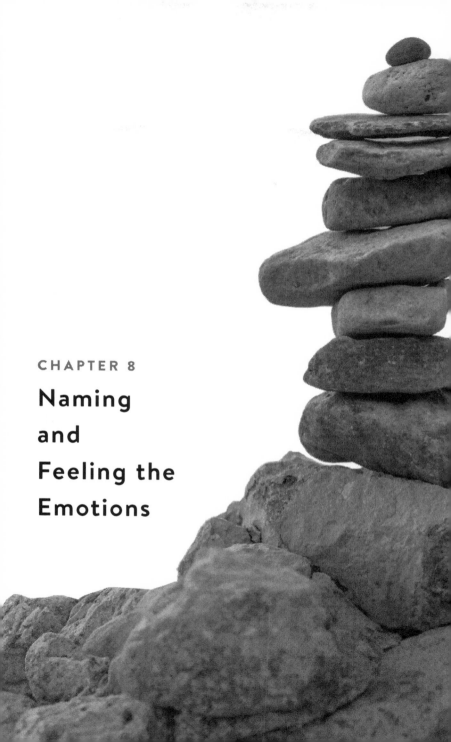

CHAPTER 8

Naming and Feeling the Emotions

"**I**'m just not a very emotional person." Someone said this to me after I'd spoken at an event about emotional health.

"Me either," I said.

She was surprised. While it might seem like someone who speaks on the topic of emotional health and writes books on grief processing has always been very in touch with their emotions, for me that's not true at all.

Feeling emotion was something I had to learn to do intentionally, and that was only after I realized that my body wouldn't let me off the hook until I did.

I didn't think I was emotional, but I knew the feeling of anxiety well.

I didn't think I was emotional, but I knew what numbness felt like.

Turns out, not processing feelings was a big root of my anxiety and numbness, especially when things "should" have felt emotionally difficult.

Your emotions may not be showing up in the obvious ways like crying or feeling intense anger, but that doesn't mean they're not there. Getting curious about them helps us to be more emotionally healthy ourselves. If we're parents, then it helps us to better know how to guide our kids to feel and understand their emotions.

Being "not very emotional" doesn't let us off the hook from getting in tune with and processing our emotions. Our body sometimes knows emotion better than our brain does.

And what's more, you cannot shut off difficult emotions without shutting off the positive ones as well. One thing I began to notice in early adulthood was my lack of feeling internally excited, joyful, and happy. Intellectually, I'd tell you that I had those emotions. I smiled and laughed, and no one would have thought I was an unhappy person, but inwardly, I didn't actually *feel* any of those happy emotions.

As Brené Brown says, "We can't selectively numb emotion.

Numb the dark and you numb the light."[21]

It was great to not feel many difficult emotions, but that superpower also meant forfeiting the ability to feel the positive emotions as well. As a new mom at the time, I remember looking down at my baby girl and thinking, "I don't want to miss out on *feeling* all of the good moments. I don't want to be numb to the joys of motherhood."

In order to process hard things from the past or difficult things as they arise in the present, we have to be able to feel *and* intellectually process. This requires both sides of our brain. Because most of us lean more toward one side or the other, we have to be intentional about engaging the side that feels most uncomfortable. The right side of the brain is where emotions and creativity live, and the left side is where logic, order, and mental spreadsheets live. The Unstacking Method accesses both sides of the brain because we're making space for emotional expression while doing so through a structured, systematic process.

If you tend to be more right-brained, bringing in some intellectual processing is helpful for effective unstacking. If you, like me, are more of a left-brained person, having structure enables you to feel comfortable enough to venture into the more chaotic territory of emotion.

As we discussed in the previous chapter, recognizing and wordsmithing both the unhealthy and combating narratives is where the left brain comes in. You are cognitively identifying those belief systems and creating narratives that your left brain can say when your right brain still wants to believe and live out the harmful one.

You can also cognitively name emotions for each grief block. When you create your Grief Tower Timeline, you'll go through each block and write emotion words for it. Sometimes this alone can stimulate feeling the emotion, but often you're still

---

21 Brown, B. (2010). *The gifts of imperfection.* Simon & Schuster.

using your logical left brain to decide what you felt during that experience. Naming the emotion words is important, but you also have to *feel* the emotions that led to that block on your Grief Tower being so impactful for your life. Some of us do this naturally, but for those of us who don't, bringing in some new tools can be helpful.

Some of the tools below can be done on your own, and some require professional support. All are helpful ways to move from cognitively thinking about emotions to actually feeling them.

But first, it's important to consider our current relationship with emotions and how that came to be. Unstacking emotional narratives is an important part of naming and feeling them in healthy ways. Like our narratives around relationships and ourselves, we also have narratives about emotions. Sometimes those come from our internal wiring – our personality and the way we naturally operate. Sometimes, they come from lines we were told directly or indirectly.

Here are some common narratives around feeling emotion:

"Expressing difficult emotions shows weakness."
"I'm being a baby if I cry."
"Feeling emotions like anger or anxiety is sinful."
"Feelings can't be trusted, so I should ignore them."
"All emotions are good to feel and express without limitation."
"It's selfish to focus on my emotions when the other people around me are hurting too."
"I need to suck it up and be strong."

Can you pinpoint narratives you've come to believe about emotion? Where did those come from? What causes you to keep believing them?

Recognizing how we feel about the way we feel can help us to get past the barrier that keeps us from unstacking on an emotional level. When we're grasping onto any of the narratives above, we're not going to be able to process the emotional layers of the grief and pain we've experienced in our life. Because emotions are our body's release valve, this conscious or subconscious decision will eventually be destructive, and our Grief Tower will crash. Allowing for emotional response and healing is a primary component of the unstacking process. As much as some of us would prefer it, unstacking without feeling is not a viable option.

Thankfully, there are ways for those of us who are less comfortable with feeling to learn how to experience emotions in ways that feel safer and more manageable than just letting the floodgates open. The methods below are also helpful for those of us who are more naturally inclined to feel emotion but need to channel it into productive unstacking. One of these methods may work well for you on its own, or you may find that a combination of multiple approaches is most effective for you.

Guided Imagery

Guided Imagery is a research-based approach to healing trauma and reducing stress. Many research studies have demonstrated the effectiveness of this method in reducing cortisol levels and resolving past trauma.[22] Psychologists have also deemed it safe and effective for someone to do on their own.[23]

However, if you experience any of the symptoms of distress discussed in Chapter 3 when attempting this or any of the suggestions in this book, pause and wait until you can process that block with a mental health professional. Again, if it is a specific block that produces the response, you can still keep processing. You just need to move onto a different block.

Guided imagery combines relaxation with "time-traveling"

---

22 Weigensberg MJ, Wen CKF, Spruijt-Metz D, Lane CJ. (2022). Effects of group-delivered stress-reduction guided imagery on salivary cortisol, salivary amylase, and stress mood in urban, predominantly Latino adolescents. *Glob Adv Health Med.* http://doi.org/10.1177/21649561211067443.

23 Hart, Jane. (2008). Guided imagery alternative and complementary therapies. 295-299. http://doi.org/10.1089/act.2008.14604

(mentally returning to the scene of the difficult experience). You'll begin by laying or sitting comfortably and relaxing your body through deep breathing. Some people like to begin by closing their eyes and visualizing a waterfall, ocean waves, or other peaceful environment. When you're ready, you'll watch yourself (as if you're watching a movie) go back to the incident where the trauma or difficult experience occurred. As you watch the scene unfold, you'll allow yourself to feel for the person (you) in that situation. Are you angry for them? Sad for them? Let your body experience those emotions.

Then, you'll mentally "send in" your current self – imagining that you're going into the situation to help. Go in and comfort your past self with words or actions. Some common phrases I hear when people use this method are: "It wasn't your fault," "This shouldn't have happened to you," "You're going to be okay," "When you grow up, you will have so many people who love you well," and "You won't hurt like this forever."

Allowing yourself to experience the emotions that you perhaps couldn't feel when the event took place or that you did feel but have never been able to resolve and unstack can be incredibly healing and is a huge step in unstacking the block on your Grief Tower.

EMDR

The first time I went to counseling for the traumas I had experienced in Africa, I was sitting across from the counselor recounting those traumatic experiences. I had no problem talking about them and could nonchalantly explain, in detail, the things I had gone through. At that point I would never have thought to label them as traumatic.

She asked, "When you think about that experience of watching someone be burned alive, how distressing does that feel on a scale of 1 to 10?"

"I don't know, maybe a 3?"

"A 3?"

"Yeah, like I can see how it *would* be distressing, but I don't feel anything in my body when I think about it."

"Okay, how distressing would you say it felt when you were in that moment?"

"Maybe a 4? I remember feeling sick to my stomach, but I also remember feeling numb and thinking that I must just be really tough. I've always done really well in a crisis."

"Hmmmm, interesting."

"What about Samuel's death?"

"Ummm, about the same, I guess."

I'm pretty sure it was through this conversion that the counselor realized I was going to need more than talk therapy.

The great thing about EMDR (Eye Movement Desensitization and Restoration) is that it can connect your thinking brain with your emotional brain without you having to "tap into" your emotions, which was difficult for me to do. I would get so caught up in figuring out *how* to elicit an emotional response that it would still be my left brain trying to make it happen. If the sides of my brain were talking to one another, I can imagine my right brain saying to my left brain, "You know what, you just keep taking over. That sounds way easier and safer." No amount of talking was changing my right brain's mind. EMDR created an environment where my emotional brain could be accessed without me trying to conjure up emotion.

EMDR is a well-researched method for healing from trauma and other adverse experiences. The EMDR Institute says, "Some of the studies show that 84%-90% of single-trauma victims no longer have post-traumatic stress disorder after only three 90-minute sessions." Another study, funded by the HMO Kaiser Permanente, found that 100% of the single-trauma victims and 77% of multiple trauma victims were no longer diagnosed with PTSD after only six 50-minute sessions. In another study, 77% of combat veterans were free of PTSD in 12 sessions.

There has been so much research on EMDR therapy that it is now recognized as an effective form of treatment for trauma and other disturbing experiences by organizations such as the American Psychiatric Association, the World Health Organization, and the Department of Defense."[24]

EMDR is essentially Guided Imagery but with external stimuli and repeated processing of the same event in small doses. The basis for its effectiveness is in the bilateral brain stimulation (stimulating both the right and left side of your brain) that occurs while revisiting past trauma and is administered by stimulating alternating sides of your body. The therapist may do this by instructing you to follow an object or light that's moving back and forth with your eyes, holding a vibrating paddle in each hand that vibrates back and forth, or wearing headphones that make a beeping sound in alternating ears (or other similar techniques).

When we're working with clients and there's a block on their Grief Tower that either seems too distressing to process on their own, or they're unable to tap into their emotions and feel anything about a block, EMDR is a form of therapy we often recommend.

Trauma-Informed Yoga

The mindfulness and stretching hallmarks of yoga have been found to be incredibly healing for those who have experienced trauma. Yoga therapist Paul Brown says, "It doesn't have to be a major event in someone's life. It can be just something gradual — something insidious — that just slowly seeps in and you don't even realize it. Then, at some point, you realize that you don't feel good and you're not sure why. That's trauma."[25]

Because trauma is stored in the body, a body-focused practice like yoga can be an effective way of feeling and releasing the

---

24 EMDR Institute, Inc. *For Clinicians.* https://www.emdr.com/what-is-emdr/

25 Cleveland Clinic. (n.d.). How yoga can help heal trauma: The healing benefits of trauma-informed practices. Retrieved September 1, 2023, from https://health.clevelandclinic.org/trauma-informed-yoga

emotion of the trauma from your body.

A study facilitated by Bessel van der Kolk (the author of *The Body Keeps the Score*) and a team of researchers found that trauma-informed yoga significantly reduced the symptoms of post-traumatic stress disorder (PTSD). The outcomes were comparable to other well-researched psychological methods.[26]

Trauma-informed yoga can be helpful for both those who lean more right-brained *and* those who lean more left-brained. If you're having difficulty getting in touch with the emotions of your grief block, trauma-informed yoga can help to find and release those. On the flipside, if you're having difficulty finding language to intellectually process your grief block, the yoga practice can lead to a reconnection of the pathways in your brain that are needed to bring words to your experience.

You can find trauma-informed yoga classes offered in your area or virtually by searching "Trauma Informed Yoga" or "Trauma Sensitive Yoga" online.

Other Methods

Some other ways that can be helpful for finding and feeling the emotions associated with a Grief Tower block are:

- Write a letter that you'll never send to the person who caused the grief block experience. A good starting place can be asking yourself, "Why did that feel so hard?" and then articulating why their actions or response or lack of response was so impactful.
- Watch an emotional movie. When you begin to feel emotions about the movie, shift your focus to your Grief Tower block and ask yourself, "What made that feel

26 Van der Kolk BA, Stone L, West J, Rhodes A, Emerson D, Suvak M, Spinazzola J. (2014). Yoga as an adjunctive treatment for posttraumatic stress disorder: A randomized controlled trial. *J Clin Psychiatry.* 75(6) https://www.doi.org/10.4088/JCP.13m08561. PMID: 25004196.

so hard?" With your emotional brain already online with the help of the movie, you may have an easier time transferring the emotions to your Grief Block.

- Try acupuncture or massage. Both cause the body to relax and release tension, and when this happens, stored up emotions can also be released. There are even "Emotional Release Sessions" advertised with both of these therapies. It may feel awkward or uncomfortable, especially if you don't tend to be an emotionally expressive person, but it can be greatly beneficial to have a grief block in mind, go through a massage or acupuncture session, and allow your emotions about that grief block to surface during or after your session. Sometimes your body just needs to relax before you can feel the ability to release emotion.

After you've completed your Grief Tower Timeline and are ready to begin processing each block, you may choose to come back to this chapter for ideas for the emotional processing part of the unstacking process.

Exercise #1: What narratives have you historically had about emotions? Where did those come from?

Exercise #2: If you struggle with allowing yourself to feel difficult emotions, what can you tell yourself as a reminder that naming and feeling emotions is good and important?

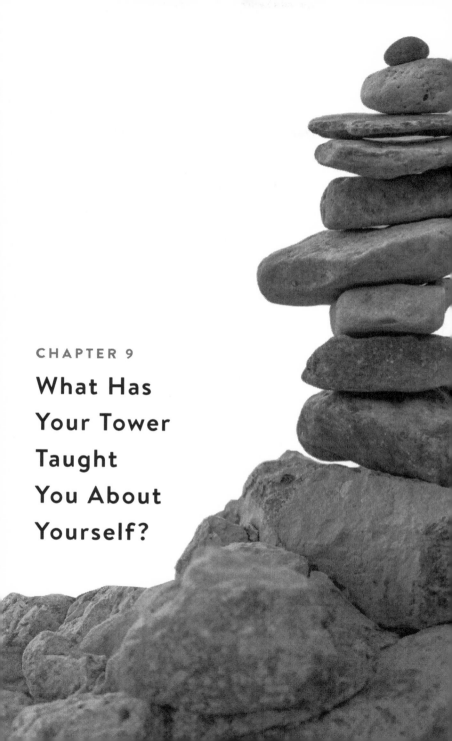

CHAPTER 9

What Has Your Tower Taught You About Yourself?

As humans, we're always trying to make sense of the world and of our experiences. We want reasons and explanations, truth and understanding. When hard things happen, one of the first things we seek to figure out is why that happened to us. This is where our internal narratives about ourselves are born.

Few things influence our opinion of ourselves more than our Grief Tower blocks. Sometimes these come indirectly through our own interpretation of the difficult situation and our part in it. But other times, these narratives are spoken over us, giving verbal confirmation to what we were already perceiving to be true.

Some common narratives about ourselves are:

"I'm too needy."
"I need to be strong."
"I have to be perfect."
"I'm the rebel."
"I'm irresponsible."
"I'm a disappointment."
"I'm responsible."
"I'm too sensitive."
"I need to set an example."
"I'm not likable."
"I'm unlovable."
"I'm a burden."
"I'm not like everyone else."
"I'm going to mess something up."

As you can see, these are not all negative. In difficult circumstances, positive narratives can also arise. But even the positive ones can be unhelpful if you're unaware of what they are and how you're using them.

For example, consider the "I'm responsible" narrative. In a podcast episode entitled "Role Reversal: When a Child Becomes the Parent," the guest shares her story of being the oldest in a family of six children. She recounts a typical day at six years of age: cooking, cleaning, changing diapers, reading the toddlers to sleep, and then climbing into bed exhausted at the end of the night. She describes her parents as loving and caring, but she also knew how much her responsible helpfulness was valued. She was responsible because she had to be.[27]

In and of itself, the "I'm responsible" narrative isn't bad. But in this case, it came from an unhealthy environment. If I were working through her Grief Tower with her, I would have her write the narrative down, and then we would talk about the ways it has served her. We would also look at the ways her narrative hasn't been helpful.

For example, she might say, "I'm really good at noticing what needs to be done and doing it." That's a valuable skill that certainly came from some difficult parts of her upbringing!

But when the narrative veers into, "It's my responsibility to care for everyone else's needs at the expense of my own," that's when it starts to get unhealthy.

The next question I ask is, "What happens if you keep living into that?" She might answer with:

- "I'd be chronically exhausted."
- "People wouldn't learn to take care of their own needs."
- "I won't know how to meet my own needs."

Issues arise when these thought patterns go unchecked. When we believe, either consciously or subconsciously, that "this is who I am," we begin collecting evidence to prove that to be true.

Counselor and colleague of mine, Jessi Bullis, likes to use the analogy of basketball free throws. If your narrative is, "I'm getting better at basketball!" and you throw ten free throws

---

27 Young, Adam (host). *Role reversal: When a child becomes the parent.* [Audio podcast]. The Place We Find Ourselves.

and miss five of them, you think, "Sweet! I got half of them in!" Then you keep working to be able to shoot all ten without a miss.

If your narrative is, "I'm terrible at basketball," and you throw ten free throws and miss five of them, you think, "See, I told you I was terrible! I only got half in! Basketball clearly isn't for me."

Nothing about the situation changed except the narrative. Believing the narrative to be true turns into acting on that belief, and that's where problems can arise.

There are almost always positive, helpful versions and harmful, unhelpful versions of the same internal narrative. But without naming what your narratives are and knowing what helpful and harmful versions look like, it's difficult to be intentional about the directions they lean toward. Harmful narratives are usually created to keep ourselves under control ("I need to be cautious") or to try to control others ("They just need to...").

Here are some examples of helpful vs. harmful versions of the same narrative.

"I'm too needy."
Helpful: "I know how to rely on and trust people."
Harmful (controlling self): "I know I'm too needy, so I need to be extra careful not to ask for things so people don't think that about me."
Harmful (controlling others): "They knew I was needy when they agreed to be my friend, so they're just going to have to deal with it."

"I am strong."
Helpful: "Feeling emotions and acknowledging my limits is strength."
Harmful (controlling self): "I need to always be strong and never show emotion or weakness."
Harmful (controlling others): "They need to rely on me because they won't survive without me."

"I'm the rebel."

   Helpful: "I'm not afraid to question the status quo."

   Harmful (controlling self): "I need to prove that I'm trustworthy/responsible/reliable/etc."

   Harmful (controlling others): "I don't care what anyone thinks, I'll do what I want."

"I'm too sensitive"

   Helpful: "I'm not afraid of emotion, and I can experience and express my emotions in healthy ways."

   Harmful (controlling self): "I need to keep my emotions in check so that no one thinks I'm too sensitive."

   Harmful (controlling others): "People know I'm sensitive, so they need to tread lightly."

FINDING IDENTITY IN OUR NARRATIVES

I like being strong, capable, even-keeled, ever-patient, and kind. Those traits are part of my identity and, if I'm honest, are part of how I want to be seen by the people around me. Many of those traits can also be traced back to Grief Tower blocks in which I had to be those things because I had no choice. Some, like my ability to turn off emotion and respond to the most stressful situations with a calm and patient demeanor, came from my need to disassociate and care for everyone around me when the world seemed to be crashing down.

As we begin to unstack our Grief Tower, we sometimes realize that we have an attachment to some of our narratives. We don't actually want to change them.

I like that *"I'm strong and capable."* That narrative seemed to be working well for me, and the number of times I'd been called Superwoman kept feeding my need to hold onto that identity. I liked the impressiveness of my ultra calm, capable self.

But then I kept living into that narrative. I started a company while moving across the country with two toddlers during a global pandemic. I grew the company, tried to be present with my kids, kept the house clean, moved states again, traveled to speaking events around the world, kept growing the company – all while maintaining what my colleague calls my "Disney princess demeanor." At least on the outside. On the inside, anxiety started to brew under the surface again. The more I juggled, the more it filled my insides, slowly overtaking all the crevices like spray foam insulation.

Sometimes I could keep it at bay by checking something off my to-do list – productivity wins again! But curbing anxiety by playing a game of whack-a-mole with a task list that never seemed to actually decrease became increasingly exhausting. The solution of working harder wasn't particularly effective.

Meanwhile, I'm teaching all around the world about the Grief Tower and narratives and unhealthy coping. Having done my own unstacking years ago, I was surprised to find an old narrative ("I'm strong and capable") pretending to be helpful and good but actually wreaking havoc under the surface.

When we lived in Oregon, I had a small vegetable garden that I loved. One spring I planted some flowers in the garden as well, imagining that I'd cut beautiful bouquets to put on the kitchen table. I was excited when one of those flowers took off and began to quickly grow taller. Before long it was nearly as tall as me. I would water the flowers, paying special attention to this one, and wonder what beautifulness it would bloom into. One day, a good friend of mine came into the backyard with me to water the garden. Before she even stepped off the back porch, she said, "Wow, you've got a crazy tall weed growing in there!"

"What!? That's not a weed, it's a flower!" I said.

She took me over and explained to me that it was, in fact, a weed that I had been lovingly tending for weeks.

The narrative, *"I'm strong and capable,"* seemed to be good. I thought it was a strength, something that was serving me and everyone else. And many times it was. After all, my company was thriving, my house was clean, and my children felt loved and cared for. But without healthy limits, it was only causing me to run faster, push harder, and take on more, all while putting on a persona of grace, poise, and unlimited patience. No wonder my anxiety had skyrocketed. It may have worked for a time, but it certainly wasn't sustainable.

Sometimes our narratives about ourselves seem helpful. There might be nothing inherently wrong or unhealthy about them. Sometimes we don't even realize right away that they *are* narratives. But as that narrative keeps growing, it becomes obvious whether it's healthy for us and the people around us, or whether it's a weed that's just been posing as a flower. I find that it's often the narratives that have a deep tie to who we think we are or how we want others to see us that disguise themselves.

As you're looking at your own narratives, consider narratives about your identity. What do people praise you for? What do you like about yourself? Those may be healthy and helpful as is. Or perhaps they are healthy to a point, but not if they are taken to an extreme or are maintained over a long period of time. Being aware of these narratives can help signal us in the moments or seasons when they are acting more like a weed in our garden than we had expected.

Exercise #1: Brainstorm any narratives about your identity that came to mind as you read and contemplated this chapter.

Exercise #2: How have those beliefs been confirmed by the Grief Tower blocks in your life?

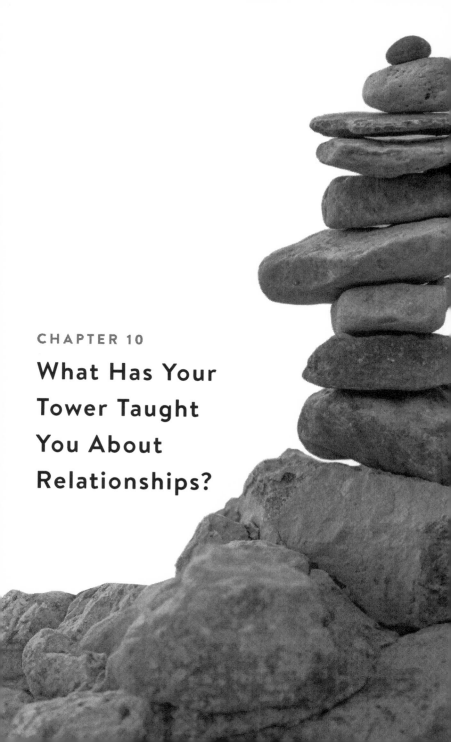

CHAPTER 10

What Has Your Tower Taught You About Relationships?

As my Grief Tower grew during our time in Africa and the year that followed, I quickly learned that the most effective coping method, along with napping and getting lost in books, was to decide that I was invincible and could handle anything. As a teenager, I developed the incredibly helpful (but not unharmful) skill of being able to turn off my emotion switch and not feel anything.

Well, almost anything. By now, you've likely caught onto the fact that the price for turning off my emotions was always a lurking anxiety - though I never learned to name it until I started unstacking my own Grief Tower.

In my teenage years when the house felt tense or heated conversations were happening around me, I learned that if I could shut down my feelings and turn my focus on everyone else, I could lighten the household mood by skillfully reducing the tension in the room, mediating arguments, or being the perfect child so I wouldn't add to the chaos. This system seemed to benefit me and everyone else, and I was constantly praised for my mature, responsible, even-keeled ways.

Fast forward five years to a newly married twenty-year-old. Aaron will tell you that he's the emotional one in our relationship. He will also tell you that in those first few years of marriage, his high-strung, "Type A" personality filled our home to the brim with tension. Good thing I knew what to do with that! Enter, invincible me with the capacity to handle all the things and go above and beyond in caring for my husband, home, and eventually children when they came along, so that his tension would decrease and I would feel better. I knew this dance well and believed I could keep it up eternally.

And I did for several years. But then my anxiety (which I had learned to name along the way) kept increasing, and I couldn't pinpoint why. So I went to counseling again. I thought I was going to address my anxiety. I certainly didn't expect to uncover unhealthy relational patterns. But as our sessions went on, I began to discover that the narratives I was believing might actually have been the root of the problem.

Conversations with my therapist would go something like this:

"And you think it's your responsibility to care for the emotions of the people around you?"

"Yes, of course it is! How else would we all survive?"

 "Why do you need to be the one to carry the load of all the practical things and all the emotional things?"

"Because I can handle more than they can, and it's the kind thing to do."

"What happens if you don't do that?"

"Everything falls apart, and I'm an anxious mess."

Do you see the relational narratives that were slowly being mined out?

"It's my responsibility to care for everyone else's emotions."
"I can handle more than most people, so I should take on more."
"Kindness = taking responsibility for everyone."
"If I don't take care of everything and everyone, everything will fall apart."

Several years ago, if you would have read those narratives to me and asked if I felt they were true, I would have said, "Absolutely, 1000%." My life seemed to have proved it.

And that's the thing. With relational narratives, we tend to have a track record that proves our narrative correct.

But "seemingly correct" does not mean healthy or helpful.

Unhelpful narratives always bring with them feelings of pain, fear, anxiety, shame, desperation, and/or insecurity.

If you look at a relational narrative and imagine living it out in increasing amounts over the next decade, it never leads to a healthier relationship. The feelings that typically come to mind when you imagine living into one of these relational beliefs long term are exhaustion, resentment, bitterness, anger, and hatred.

Living into narratives around relationships usually leads to self-fulfilling prophecies. We begin to act on the beliefs we have and let the beliefs convince us that we should push people away before they get too close, end a relationship before the other person does, and protect ourselves by never trusting anyone.

The saddest part of this is that we miss out on the healing and growth we can find in relationships. Isolation never leads to increased health. In fact, isolation and loneliness have been shown to lead to heart disease, depression, and cognitive decline.[28] One study even found that the long-term health outcomes of loneliness were equivalent to smoking 15 cigarettes a day.[29] Health and poor relationships will always be in contradiction.

While loneliness decreases our well-being, healthy relationships increase our health in all areas. A study looking at the correlation between relational experiences and physical health found that fewer negative relational experiences predicted lower stress, better coping, and better physiological functioning in daily life, such as lower blood pressure and a healthy heart rate.[30]

Part of unstacking our Grief Tower is looking into our relationships and how their health has been impacted by relational hardship in our past. The reason for this is twofold: we want to have healthy relationships going forward, which requires unstacking the narratives that would prevent healthy

28 National Institute on Aging. (n.d.). *Loneliness and social isolation — Tips for staying connected* Retrieved August 23, 2023 from https://www.nia.nih.gov/health/loneliness-and-social-isolation-tips-staying-connected#:~:text=Studies%20show%20that%20loneliness%20and,be%20socially%20isolated%20or%20lonely.

29 Holt-Lunstad J, Smith TB, Layton JB. (2010). Social relationships and mortality risk: A meta-analytic review. *PLoS Med,* 7(7). https://doi.org/10.1371/journal.pmed.1000316

30 Don, B. P., Gordon, A. M., & Berry Mendes, W. (2023). The good, the bad, and the variable: Examining stress and blood pressure responses to close relationships. *Social Psychological and Personality Science*, 0(0). https://doi.org/10.1177/19485506231156018

functioning, and we also need people in our life who know and love us well enough to walk with us through future hardship so future grief blocks don't continue to stack.

PROTECTIVE NARRATIVES

I was working with a client who was sent to boarding school in a different country at age seven. The staff at the boarding school was not nurturing at best and cruel at worst. When she returned home for school holidays, her parents were always too busy to spend time with her, so she spent her days taking care of herself. While she had friends over the years, she never let herself have needs and always held people at arm's length.

From as early as she could remember, she realized, "I have to look out for myself because no one else will."

This grew into:

"I can't have needs."
"I can't rely on anyone."
"I can't trust anyone to truly care for me or about me."

She had purposefully constructed these narratives to protect herself. I asked her what feelings come to mind when she thinks about her life through the lens of these narratives.

"Lonely. So lonely."

While the narratives were developed to protect herself, they won't bring her a full life with healthy relationships. Protection doesn't mean thriving. Healthy relationships require the risk of not living into your relational narratives. That feels scary, but ultimately, it will lead to being able to feel known and loved, which is something we all long for – even if we don't believe we need it. (Could that be another internal narrative?)

As we begin to uncover relational narratives, we begin to understand how and why we operate in relationships the way that we do. And sometimes it is very purposeful and intentional. For example, I went straight from Africa to college in Indiana. When I first started the semester, I was eager to jump in and make friends.

However, the wildly different cultures of rural Indiana and my international friend group in Africa seemed to be an exhausting barrier to developing deep friendships. It felt like every time I opened my mouth that first semester, the words I spoke didn't get the reaction I was expecting. My attempts to be funny were met with awkward smiles. My attempts to deepen relationships by sharing about something a bit more vulnerable were met with comments that communicated a lack of ability to relate to my experiences and no invitation to continue the conversation.

I remember thinking, "I'll only be here long enough to get my degree anyway, and it will be easier to leave if I never make close friends." I knew what it felt like to leave close friends, so when my initial attempts to build relationships didn't work, that seemed like a good excuse to stop trying. After all, "Having friends isn't worth the pain of losing them when it's time to leave."

In the three years that followed, Aaron and I dated, and he became my closest friend. His guy friends became my friends, and we would all hang out and have a great time. But my female friendships remained casual. Deep conversations or the possibility of lifelong friendship seemed like a lost cause. The narrative, "It will be easier to leave if I never make close friends," was a great excuse to stop trying and to decide that I didn't need good friends anyway. It was a purposeful and intentional narrative.

Perhaps the relational narratives you've lived by are the ones that you, like me, defaulted to because it was easier than feeling hurt, pain, or disappointment. You put it in place as a self-protective measure to keep you safe from the pain that would be possible if you were to hope for more. One of the only ways we get out of a harmful relational narrative is realizing that living out that narrative is more risky than changing the narrative and stepping into relationships in a different way. That shift feels scary, vulnerable, and maybe like an overall terrible idea.

But what happens if you don't change?

As our odometer clicked up the miles across the country during our Indiana-to-Oregon move, a realization hit me. We were leaving someplace we'd lived for four years, and there wasn't a single person whom I was going to miss or who was going to miss me. There were no tearful goodbyes, long hugs, or goodbye parties. We just left. I remember thinking, "I did this to protect myself, but somehow this feels so much worse."

I decided that even though I had no idea how long we would live in Oregon, I wasn't going to do that again. I would figure out how to build deep friendships because the next time I moved, I wanted to have built a life that felt hard to leave.

We lived in Oregon for six years, and to be honest, the first couple of years of trying to build friendships were awkward and uncomfortable. But I kept telling myself, "Deep friendships are worth it, so keep trying." Over time, the friendship-building muscle grew stronger, and I began to develop deeper and deeper friendships.

In February of 2020, Aaron was offered a job in South Carolina, and though I hated admitting it, we knew without a doubt that we needed to go. We were sent off with a goodbye party of over 30 close friends who knew us deeply and loved us dearly. These were the same friends who'd brought food after our babies were born and whom we'd cried with when life threw hard things their way or ours. Friends who knew my kid's cute little toddler phrases and who could encourage me better than anyone or call me out when I needed a shift in perspective.

Some of these friends wrote me letters to be opened in each of the states we would drive through on our way across the country. As we drove and I opened the letters one by one, I realized that I had done it. I had made those deep friendships that I had set out to, and while leaving them and our life in Oregon hurt like hell, it was a healthy hurt. A hurt that came because what was being left was worth being sad about.

Relational narratives that developed out of our Grief Tower often set the stage for how we engage emotionally and practically with people going forward. Because they were birthed out of pain, it makes sense that we want to avoid that. But a full life where we are loved and where people love us is a risk that is worth the potential hurt. Hurt may come if we try, but loneliness is guaranteed if we don't.

Common narratives around relationships are:

- "I'm not allowed to have needs."
- "I'm annoying and bothersome to people."
- "I don't deserve love."
- "People always leave."
- "People always let you down."
- "I can't trust anyone."
- "People aren't safe."
- "Nobody likes me."
- "I'm going to mess this up."
- "As soon as they get to know me, they won't like me."
- "I'm unlovable."

Do any of these feel true to you? Are there others that you can easily name? Sometimes finding the relational narratives begins with looking at our Grief Tower blocks and seeing what narratives may have come from those. Other times, it starts with putting language to the narrative and then tracing back to see if there's a grief block it may have stemmed from.

I could have pretty easily verbalized the reason I hadn't made close friends in Indiana: "It will be easier to leave if I never make close friends." But I had to look deeper to see how that narrative came directly from the five blocks on my Grief Tower that involved me leaving my closest friends or them leaving me.

As you consider how your past has impacted your relational narratives, explore it from both angles. Look at the narratives that feel true to you and see if there's something in your past that birthed that narrative, and look at the hard things in the past to see if there are narratives that came out of those that perhaps you wouldn't have noticed or named on their own.

Exercise #1: Brainstorm any relational narratives of yours that came to mind as you read and contemplated this chapter.

Exercise #2: How have those beliefs been confirmed by the Grief Tower blocks in your life?

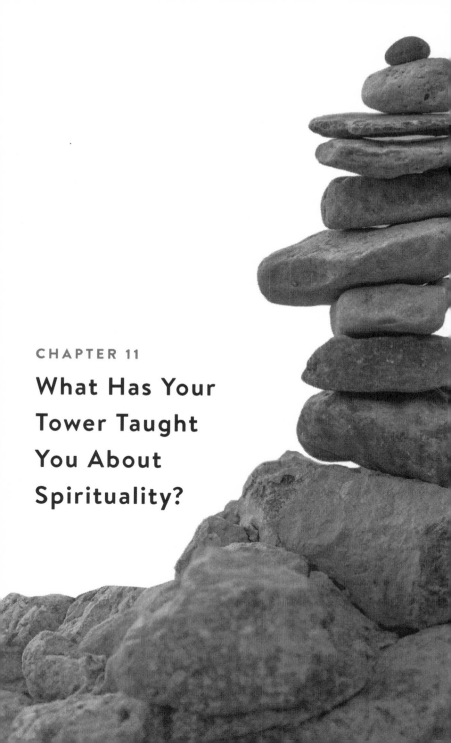

CHAPTER 11

What Has Your Tower Taught You About Spirituality?

"I didn't even know if God existed, but if He did, I was angry at him."

—*Unstacking client*

Whether or not you believe *in* God, you do believe something *about* God. You may believe he exists or doesn't,
is kind and loving or is distant and uncaring, is the
author of life or has nothing to do with the earth we live on
and the air we breathe.

These beliefs came from somewhere, and they've morphed
throughout your life into what they are today. None of us has the
exact perspective and beliefs on spirituality that we did when
we were two years old because we didn't have the cognition at
two to develop thoughts and opinions on the matter.

Where, then, did our beliefs about the spiritual world (or
lack thereof) come from?

Sometimes they came from the people around us – the
grandmother who took us to church or the parent who taught
us that God was a farce. But at some point, most of us grow out
of just taking someone's word for it, and we begin to develop
our own opinions.

The more I've worked with people unstacking their Grief
Towers, the more I'm convinced that the majority of foundational beliefs we have about spirituality were birthed out of
the blocks on our Grief Tower.

For some people, the hardest things in life were met with
the felt presence of a loving God, and that convinced them that
not only is God undeniably real, but they can't imagine going
through the next hard thing without his presence and comfort.

For others, the more difficult blocks on their Grief Tower
convinced them that there must not be a God or that if there
is, he must not care. Otherwise that horrible thing wouldn't
have happened.

For those who have historically had a spiritual background
but haven't been practicing in recent history, I find that the

reason is often because of how they believe God showed up during their hardest moments or how God shows up when hard things happen now. It can be easy to assign blame to a deity whom we feel hasn't shown up with care and compassion at the times we needed it most.

WHY DOES SPIRITUALITY MATTER?

One of the reasons that looking at how your Grief Tower has impacted your spiritual life, or lack thereof, is important is because spirituality has been consistently linked to resilience by researchers.

When something feels terrifying, distressing, or stressful, our brain signals our adrenal glands to pump cortisol. Our brain also pumps something called dehydroepiandrosterone, or most commonly DHEA. DHEA protects the brain from the harmful ramifications of too much cortisol. This means that the more the DHEA levels rise during a stressful event, the more the brain is protected from cortisol and the better the function and long-term health. In other words, a brain that has more DHEA secreted along with the cortisol is more resilient to hardship, not just in the moment, but also to the long-term effects of stress on the body.

This is one of the reasons why some people who experience traumas in their developmental years have negative health outcomes in adulthood, while others do not. It is likely due to the ratio of DHEA to cortisol that their brain experienced during those adverse experiences.

What researchers have found is that there are certain things that contribute to DHEA production. In a study done by Fuller School of Theology, correlational analyses found that Spirituality (e.g., "My life is enriched by my spiritual beliefs, practices, and/or experiences") was significantly correlated with the DHEA/cortisol ratio being at a strong level. They also found that the

DHEA level was impacted more by spirituality than by Adaptive Engagement (e.g., "I can adapt to changing circumstances"), Sense of Purpose (e.g., "I find meaning in my work"), and Life Satisfaction (e.g., "I am lucky to be able to do the work I do").[31]

Other research also showed a correlation between a healthier cortisol to DHEA ratio and spiritual meditation.[32]

There is little research on what exactly it is about spirituality that contributes to resilience, but some of the things I have heard from those I've worked with are:

- Feeling that they are a part of a bigger, purposeful story
- Feeling a supernatural peace and comfort when they spend time in prayer
- Relying on scripture for comfort through hardship, sometimes using scripture as combating narratives
- Believing that there's a higher power who will work things out for good in the end
- A spiritual focus on forgiveness helps them to move past a grief block more easily

Another study by Columbia University looked at spirituality's impact on neurology. They found that participating in regular meditation or other spiritual practices actually thickens parts of the brain's cortex, providing a potential explanation for why those who practice activities are less prone to depression, even if they are genetically predisposed to it..[33]

31 Fuller Studio. (n.d.). Spirituality: *A facet of resilience.* Retrieved September 9, 2023 from https://fullerstudio.fuller.edu/spirituality-a-facet-of-resilience/

32 T. E. Seeman, L. F. Dubin, And M. Seeman. (2003). Religiosity/ Spirituality and health: A critical review of the evidence for biological pathways. *American Psychologist,* 58(1), 53–63.

33 Miller L, Bansal R, Wickramaratne P, et al. (2014). Neuroanatomical correlates of religiosity and spirituality: A study in adults at high and low familial risk for depression. *JAMA Psychiatry.* 71(2):128–135. https://www.doi.org/10.1001/jamapsychiatry.2013.3067

Whether or not spirituality is present in your daily life, evaluating how it has been impacted by your Grief Tower can help you to see if your decisions to seek out or avoid spiritual practices have been impacted by the blocks on your tower. No matter what your Grief Tower has taught you about spirituality, you may decide that the research about its benefits makes it a practice worth exploring.

A SPIRITUAL MEDITATION

One of the most powerful meditations I've seen when using the Unstacking Method is praying through a grief block. I've seen both people of faith and those skeptical about the idea find comfort and healing through a meditation session that goes something like this:

God, we come before you with this hurt that [name] experienced. She/he felt [list emotions] and is now feeling [list emotions].

As we sit here and remember this [event/experience/hardship], would you show him/her where you were when that was happening?

I ask them to picture the event/experience/hardship like it's a movie playing in their mind. Then they ask God to show them where he was during that time.

I ask them if there are any questions that they want to ask God about that block and invite them to do so.

I pause, and we sit in silence.

When they're ready, I ask them what they saw, heard, and felt. Sometimes it's a feeling of overwhelming peace. Sometimes it's a realization that they hadn't had before. Other times, it's a clear picture of God with them during their grief experience.

This is something that you can do on your own. Whether

or not you believe in God or consider yourself religious, this meditation and other spiritual practices can be an effective way of finding healing and building resilience for the future hardships that come.

GRATITUDE

The spiritual discipline of gratitude can be an important piece of unstacking and healing.

Gratitude has been shown to reduce depression[34] and even improve physical health like blood pressure.[35] One study involving nearly 300 adults sought to see if simply writing letters of gratitude would improve mental wellbeing. The participants were divided into three groups, and all participants received counseling services. One group wrote one letter of gratitude to another person each week for three weeks, another group wrote their deepest thoughts and feelings about their negative emotions and experiences, and the third group did nothing in addition to the counseling.

The group who wrote the letters of gratitude reported significantly better mental health outcomes four weeks after the writing period ended. Even more incredible, a brain scan was done on participants three months after the study ended and found that those who had written gratitude letters showed greater activation in the medial prefrontal cortex than those who did not. This indicates that the practice of gratitude may

34 Iodice J., Malouff J., Schutte N,. (2021). The association between gratitude and depression: A meta-analysis. *Int J Depress Anxiety, (4),* https://www.doi.org/10.23937/2643-4059/1710024

35 Jans-Beken Phd, Lilian & Jacobs, Nele & Janssens, Mayke & Peeters, Sanne & Reijnders, Jennifer & Lechner, Lilian & Lataster, Johan. (2019). Gratitude and health: An updated review. *The Journal of Positive Psychology.* 1-40. https://www.doi.org/10.1080/17439760.2019.1651888.

even have lasting effects on the brain.[36]

Whether thanking God, the universe, or another person, integrating gratitude into the unstacking process can be a helpful combination for healing. When doing this, we want to notice if we're tempted to jump to gratitude as a way to avoid processing difficult emotions and instead learn how to hold both in tandem.

Here are some ways this could look:

- Writing letters of gratitude to those who cared for and supported you during some of your Grief Tower experiences
- Listing strengths that you're grateful for that came out of difficult experiences
- Expressing thankfulness for survival and/or for the life you're living now
- Using the ampersand (&) method: draw an ampersand in the middle of a page and, thinking about one Grief Tower block, write all the reasons why that block was so difficult on one side of the page and anything good that came from it on the other side of the page

Gratitude shouldn't be misunderstood as being grateful that the hard thing happened. There are horrors in life that shouldn't be sugar coated. Instead, we're recognizing that while we may wish it had never happened, we can mine out something good that came from it. What good thing would not be in your life, or what character traits would you not possess to the extent that you now do, if that hard thing hadn't happened?

---

36 Wong, J., Owen, J., Gabana, N., Brown, J., McInnis, S.,Toth, P. & Gilman, L. (2018). Does gratitude writing improve the mental health of psychotherapy clients? Evidence from a randomized controlled trial, *Psychotherapy Research*, (28)2, 192-202, https://www.doi.org/10.1080/10503307.2016.1169332

PRAYER

Prayer is the exercise of talking to a divine being. It can happen verbally or internally, privately or corporately, and is most often associated with a monotheistic (one-God) belief system. Research has continually shown the positive impact of prayer practices on mental health. A study done on 44 participants looked at the impact of six weekly one-hour prayer sessions on depression and anxiety. Not only did the participants' depression and anxiety reduce after the six weeks of prayer sessions, but a repeat evaluation one year later showed that the prayer sessions had lasting effects on their mental health. They showed "significantly less depression and anxiety, more optimism, and greater levels of spiritual experience than the baseline (pre-prayer) measures."[37]

Whether or not prayer is correlated with improved mental health outcomes is largely impacted by our perception of God. This is one of the reasons the process of understanding what our narratives about God are and how they came to be is important. Research found that those who pray frequently to a God they "perceive as a secure attachment figure derive clear mental health benefits, while those who pray to a God who is perceived as distant or unresponsive experience elevated levels of anxiety-related symptoms."[38]

Prayer as a spiritual practice has the potential to lead to positive mental health outcomes, but the determining factor in this is our narratives about God and how those narratives impact the nature of our relationship with a divine being.

37 Boelens P., Reeves R., Replogle W., Koenig H. (2012). The effect of prayer on depression and anxiety: maintenance of positive influence one year after prayer intervention. Int J Psychiatry Med. 43(1), 85-98. https://www.doi.org/10.2190/PM.43.1.f. PMID: 22641932.

38 Ellison, C., Bradshaw, M., Flannelly, K, & Galek, K. (2014). Prayer, attachment to God, and symptoms of anxiety-related disorders among U.S. adults. Sociology of Religion. 75. 208-233. https://www.doi.org/10.1093/socrel/srt079.

Exercise #1: What have your Grief Tower blocks taught you about spirituality? How has that impacted your spiritual practices or lack thereof?

Exercise #2: Try one of the spiritual practices in this chapter. After doing so, reflect on how it felt, if any other narratives were brought up, and if you'd like to continue implementing that practice or others going forward.

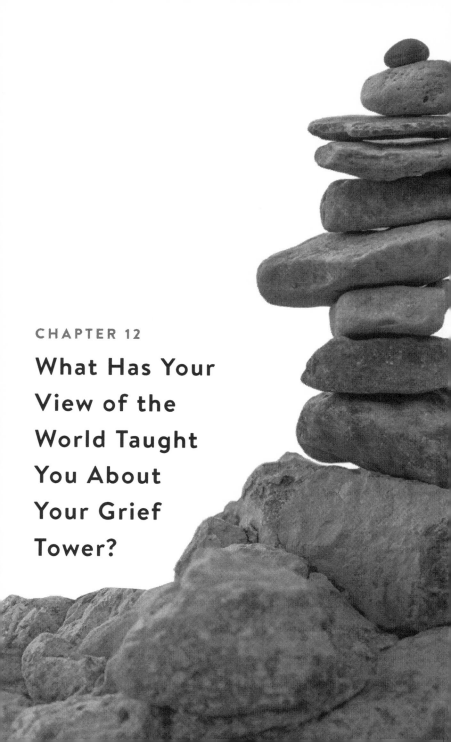

CHAPTER 12

What Has Your View of the World Taught You About Your Grief Tower?

Did you ever play with a kaleidoscope as a child? I remember being mesmerized by this small tube that looked so simple from the outside but would come to life with gorgeous colors and shapes when I looked through it. As I twisted it, the beads at the end would shift with a sound like a rainstick, creating an ever-new colorful mosaic.

When you're holding up a kaleidoscope, looking at it from the outside, you can see the beads at the end as they are in reality – simple, normal beads. But put the tube up to your eye and gaze through the mirrors in the tube, and those same beads transform into something delightful. The beads never actually changed, but your perspective of them shifted.

We all live on the earth, so technically speaking we all walk around looking at the same things. From a zoomed out, stripped down perspective, the world is like the beads at the end of the kaleidoscope when you're holding it out in front of you. Nothing is influencing your view of it, you're just seeing the beads as they are.

But none of us actually views the world that way. Instead, we all look at it through different lenses. Like the mirrors that distort the beads in the kaleidoscope, there are layers that influence how we see the world and life in general.

Unlike in the previous chapters, the relationship between our view of the world and our Grief Tower is not very clear cut. Sometimes, a Grief Tower experience will influence our view of the world, but more than our experiences, the way we see the world is largely influenced by our family and our community. Instead of the Grief Tower influencing our view of the world, our perspective of the world often influences how we view blocks on our Grief Tower.

The lens through which we see the world is also the lens through which we see the hard things that have happened in our lives. And occasionally those hard things that happen will shift our perspective like rotating the kaleidoscope.

Researcher Jeremy Clifton calls these views of the world

"primal world beliefs" – the way that we see the world and life. While there are many sub-beliefs, he distills the main beliefs down to three general categories:

- Safe vs. Dangerous
- Abundant vs. Barren
- Alive vs. Mechanic[39]

SAFE VS. DANGEROUS

Those of us who view the world as generally safe believe that true threats are few and far between. This leads to more risk-taking in the environment and being more trusting in relationships. We view the world as mostly good despite the hardship and crises that exist.

Those of us who view the world as generally dangerous tend to be more cautious in our environment and relationships. We assume that not being hyper-aware will be detrimental. We're more likely to view the world as "going downhill" and to notice the suffering of people around the world more acutely.

Safe-World Narratives
"I don't need to worry myself with scary things that probably won't happen anyway."
"It'll probably be fine."
"The world is a pretty safe place."

Dangerous-World Narratives
"I always need to be on my guard."

---

39 Clifton, J. D. W., Baker, J. D., Park, C. L., Yaden, D. B., Clifton, A. B. W., Terni, P., Miller, J. L., Zeng, G., Giorgi S., Schwartz, H. A., & Seligman, M. E. P. (2019). Primal world beliefs. *Psychological Assessment*, 31(1), 82-99. https://doi.org/10.1037/pas0000639.

"The world isn't a good place."
"Something bad is probably going to happen to me."

ABUNDANT VS. BARREN

Through the lens of abundance, we see all the things the world has to offer and generally assume that through hard work and being a good person, accessing those things is possible for most people. We believe that the world is a beautiful place and that beauty can always be found if you pay attention and look hard enough.

When we view the world as barren, we believe that there is not enough to go around and that, in general, the world is a place of scarcity. We see the world as boring, not worth exploring, and we can find ourselves wondering what the point of working hard is because we feel there's nothing truly great to aim for anyway.

Abundant-World Narratives
"Improvement is always possible."
"There's always a solution."
"Working hard and being kind pays off."

Barren-World Narratives
"I knew I shouldn't have let myself get excited. Something always happens, and I just end up being disappointed."
"I just assume the other shoe is always going to drop, so it's better to be ready for it."
"Life is more painful than pleasurable."
"The state of the world is going downhill."

ALIVE VS. MECHANIC

When we see the world as "alive," we see meaning in nearly everything. We believe that the universe is active and plays a role in how things turn out. An alive world is one where we feel that our lives have a purpose that goes beyond ourselves and that we were "destined" for that purpose.

When we see the world as mechanic, we don't believe that there is a deeper meaning behind things that happen. We view the world as a machine that doesn't have any intentions or plans.

Alive-World Narratives
"Everything happens for a reason."
"There's a purpose for my life."
"You get what you deserve."

Mechanic-World Narrative
"I can't change what's going to happen."
"There's no grand plan for the universe."
"People are interchangeable, and there aren't special roles in life that only that person can fill."

WHERE DO THESE BELIEFS COME FROM?

Researchers hypothesized that these beliefs would be heavily influenced by wealth, privilege, experience, and other economic and environmental factors, but they found that those actually had little impact on world beliefs.[40] Instead, family and community tend to set the foundation through

---

40 Kerry, N., White, K., O'Brien, M., Perry, L., Clifton, J. (2023). Despite popular intuition, positive world beliefs poorly reflect several objective indicators of privilege, including wealth, health, sex, and neighborhood safety. *Journal of Personality*. https://doi.org/10.1111/jopy.12877.

what is taught verbally and non-verbally, what is disciplined, and what is modeled.

Significant Adults

The first layer of influence for our views about the world is typically our parents or other significant adult relationships. Once I was at the park with my children, and another child was swinging while his mother stood close by. Entranced by something on her phone, she didn't see her son hop off the swing and run behind the slide. She looked up, panicked when she realized he was out of eyesight, but found him seconds later not twenty feet away from her. In her fear she grabbed his arm and said, "What were you doing?! You couldn't see me from there! Someone could have kidnapped you!"

I don't know if this fear-based reaction was a common occurrence between this boy and his mom, but her words and actions clearly communicated, "The world is unsafe. Don't leave my sight."

If she continued to model and communicate this dangerous-world perspective, her son would likely grow to adopt that view. When experiencing something scary or hearing about a tragedy, he would likely view those experiences through his dangerous-world lens and think, "See, the world isn't safe."

On the flip side, when a grandparent or other significant adult communicates things like, "There's a plan for your life," or "You have a purpose," a difficult experience might be viewed as being a part of that plan or as something that can be used for good. We see this belief play out when we hear of people using their past hardships as a way to help others. They might say, "That was hard, but there was a purpose for it. I wouldn't be able to bring healing to people who've gone through similar traumas if I hadn't experienced that too."

Views about the world, whether they communicate that the world is beautiful and should be explored or that the world is dangerous so you should always be on guard, are often planted by parents or other significant adult relationships in the child's life. Difficult things that happen are then viewed through that lens. How you have viewed the blocks on your Grief Tower may be tied to the world beliefs that were taught or modeled by the significant adults in your life.

Community

Community also contributes to our beliefs about the world. Religious communities are often constructed around worldview. In these contexts, internal narratives about the world aren't just suggested, they're taught as truth. It becomes expected that if you're a part of the community, you'll share the same internal narratives about the world. Examples might be:

"If you obey God, you'll be blessed."
"Everything happens for a reason."

The cultural environment of the community also contributes to our beliefs. Where I lived in Tanzania, there was a pervasive narrative of "There's never enough." There were never enough desks for the number of children in the classroom, never enough food for the whole family, never enough of seemingly anything.

This created a culture in which standing patiently in line for your turn was out of the question. If you stood patiently in line, there was a good chance nothing would be left for you. Instead, charging ahead like an elephant ready to trample whatever is in the way was the only reasonable solution. Parents taught their children this because of the cultural community context in which they were living.

Experiences

While it's more often significant adults and our community context that shape our view of the world and our difficult experiences, sometimes the difficult experiences are significant enough that they do twist the kaleidoscope of our perspective on life.

When this happens, it's most often due to a significant trauma during the early childhood years. The impact of the trauma on our developing nervous system influences what our body believes about the world more than what we *think* about the world. Subsequent trauma or difficult experiences will likely confirm what those earliest experiences taught us and give us narrative language for what was first a somatic experience.

SO WHAT?

Whether through our parents, community, or childhood trauma, we've developed a way of interpreting what is happening through our perspective of the world. This interpretation extends to the hard things that happen in our lives. It influences whether we say, "I knew that was going to happen. Just when things start going well, something always goes wrong," or "Everything always works out in the end. This is a bummer, but something good will come from it."

But why does this matter? What difference does it make?

Understanding how we see the world is important because it impacts how we look at our past and how we perceive difficult things that come in the future. Positive psychology is a branch of psychology that focuses on life's positive qualities. Tied to positive psychology are attributes like optimism, gratitude, and purpose. These are aligned more closely with a safe, abundant, and alive world belief.

Research has shown that optimism – assuming positive outcomes – is tied to better stress control, an increased ability to cope with traumatic events, better physical health, and even a faster recovery from medical procedures.[41] Feeling like we have a purpose in our life is associated with increased physical health[42] and psychological health.[43] And as we talked about in the previous chapter, gratitude has numerous positive health effects. Positive world beliefs (safe, abundant, alive) are also strongly linked to hope, spirituality, zest, curiosity, and leadership.

The way we view the world makes a difference. The good news is that world beliefs can be shifted, just like we can turn the kaleidoscope to see a new variation of the same beads.

Once you're aware of the world beliefs you lean toward, you can decide whether or not those beliefs are serving you well, just like you have with the narratives about yourself, relationships, and spirituality. Do you want to continue to live into these beliefs? What emotions are associated with them? Are they the kind of beliefs that you want to pass down to the young people around you?

Then begin to look for what you *want* to see, not what you automatically see. Your brain will default to the perspective that it's been wired to know and look for, so intentionality is critical if you want to begin to shift it. When you're tempted to zoom in on the ugliness in the world, look around for something beautiful. When you're thinking about all of the things that could go wrong, think about a time when things went well, or think about how much fun it could be if you took that risk and it went well.

41 Aspinwall, L., Tedeschi R, (2010). The value of positive psychology for health psychology: progress and pitfalls in examining the relation of positive phenomena to health. *Annals of Behavioral Medicine,* 39(1), 4–15. https://doi.org/10.1007/s12160-009-9153-0

42 Kim ES, Kawachi I, Chen Y, Kubzansky LD. (2017). Association between purpose in life and objective measures of physical function in older adults. *JAMA Psychiatry.* 74(10):1039–1045. https://doi.org/10.1001/jamapsychiatry.2017.2145

43 Hallford DJ, Mellor D, Cummins RA, McCabe MP. (2018). Meaning in life in earlier and later older-adulthood: Confirmatory factor analysis and correlates of the meaning in life questionnaire. *J Appl Gerontol,* 37(10), 1270-1294. https://www.doi.org/10.1177/0733464816658750.

As you begin to unstack your Grief Tower in the next chapter, consider how your view of the world has impacted – and continues to impact – the way you view the blocks on your tower or even this unstacking process in general. It may be that practicing mindfulness in how you see the world will be an important step in approaching the unstacking process.

Exercise #1: Which primal world beliefs do you most identify with?

Exercise #2: Do you have a parent or other significant adult who lives out that belief? Does the community you're a part of lean toward certain beliefs?

Exercise #3: How were your beliefs confirmed by the things that happened in your life?

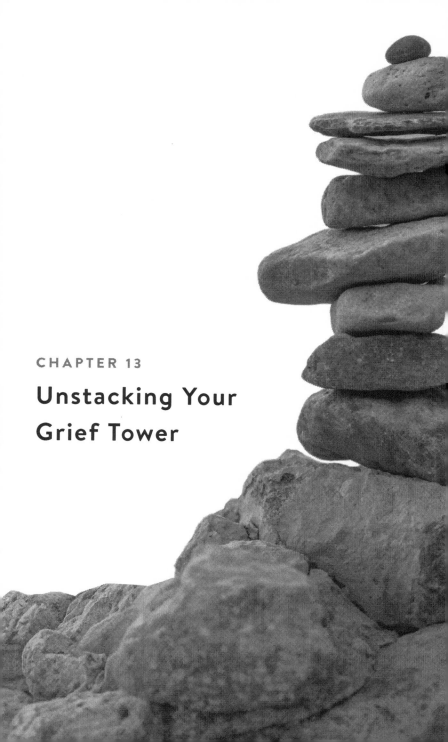

CHAPTER 13

Unstacking Your Grief Tower

WHAT IS THE GOAL?

Unstacking does not mean that we're pulling the block off our Grief Tower and throwing it over our shoulder and into the abyss, never to be seen or talked about again. Instead, we're taking it off the tower and setting it on the ground beside it. We still can go back and remember, and we can pick it up again when something reminds us of that hard thing and we just need to have a good cry. We can still notice when a pattern is surfacing again and take the time to reexamine some of our blocks. The goal of unstacking isn't to get rid of the blocks.

Neither is the goal to never deal with our internal narratives or never struggle with unhealthy coping again. That would be an impossible goal. Instead, the goal is to be aware of what our narratives are so that we notice when they slip back in and are ready with combating narratives to counteract the unhelpful ones.

Another goal of unstacking is to inspire curiosity. When you notice new patterns, new ways of coping, or new thoughts or actions and wonder, "Why do I keep doing that?" you now know how to lean in with curiosity so that you can see what they're connected to and can proactively unstack them.

PICKING UP A BLOCK AGAIN

From my earliest memories, I remember being on stage. The first time was at five years old in a purple bunny costume for a ballet production of *Winnie the Pooh*. My line was, "I love, love, LOVE carrots!" From then on, my love for musical theater, singing in church, and dancing on stage grew. Though I was very reserved off the stage, the moment I stepped into my stage-self, I blossomed.

Somewhere along the way, I began to notice that affection toward me increased with impressive performance. I would perform, and my emotional needs would be met. Though I genuinely loved starring in musicals and singing my heart out, at some point I began to tie love to performance. I began to believe things like, "I'm loved when I perform well" and "If they see me perform, they'll know I'm lovable." Naturally, this kept me seeking out ways to perform.

Over the years this focus on performance shifted from musicals to my career. In my early twenties, I entered a role where I was regularly speaking in front of groups of people, teaching content in attention-grabbing ways for hours at a time. Teaching became my performance. I loved teaching, but those same narratives also continued on. "I'm loved when I perform well, so I need to keep being impressive," I thought to myself. "People don't love *me* as much as they love my performance."

With the help of a counselor, I began to explore these narratives, the ties they had to my childhood, and the ways they impacted my daily life. Over the years, I learned to let my "performer" part take the stage when it needed to but not to let it be the whole of who I was or the part of me vying for love. I remember learning to visualize pulling out the "performer" when I needed to sing a solo or give a presentation and then putting her away and just being me.

I thought I had successfully dealt with those performance-driven narratives and thrown away the grief block of the child who needed her emotional needs met and who felt that the only way to get it was through performance. I had learned to use that performance ability when I needed it, while knowing and resting in the fact that the important people in my life loved me without performance.

Fast forward to thirty-year-old me with a growing company. I had become well known in my niche field of Third Culture Kid care, and TCK Training had become the largest company providing training and resources for that population. Anxiety had come back around, and all of my knowledge of unstacking and processing wasn't kicking it. I made an appointment with my counselor and explained my dilemma: "I'm dealing with this intense anxiety all of the sudden, and nothing I'm doing is working!"

After asking some questions, he said, "Let's go back to that performer part of you. How's she doing?"

It turns out that the old narrative ("I'm loved when I perform well, so I need to keep being impressive") had snuck back up on me. But this time, my performance wasn't on a stage. It wasn't even my keynote speaking gigs and teaching events that had sparked this anxiety. It was the ever-growing company that I was trying to run well while continuing to be impressive in every other area of my life. What I had built had become my performance.

I had begun to subconsciously worry that if I screwed it up, if I let off the gas pedal for one moment and lost momentum, if my company had a low revenue month, then everyone's love for me would be at risk – and not those people on social media that I don't actually know, but my husband, my best friends, the people I care about most. Same narrative, same struggle, different situation.

I'm not writing this book on unstacking because I've unstacked all my stuff once and for all and can now tell you how to do it because I've mastered it. I still have blocks that will resurface and need to be explored again – like the performance block I had to pick up again recently. I'm sure there will continue to be narratives and coping skills that I will be combating my whole life. Ideally it will get easier, but I don't think these things ever completely go away. They're too formative.

Again, the goal of unstacking isn't to get to a place where you've finally combated all your unhelpful narratives and are fully healed from all the hard things that have ever happened to you. Instead, it's being able to *notice* the things from our past that aren't helpful in our present and *know* what to do with them. That is the hope for all of us as we go through the process of unstacking our Grief Towers.

CREATING YOUR GRIEF TOWER TIMELINE

It's time to begin your own unstacking, starting with creating your Grief Tower Timeline. This timeline is meant to help you visualize what's on your Grief Tower and what needs to be unstacked.

Step 1 - Brainstorm
Grab a journal and write down any Grief Tower blocks that you can remember. Don't worry about explaining, processing, or even thinking about them much. Just put a word down that will remind you of that block. Use the categories below to help bring events, situations, or seasons to mind, but don't worry about it if something that you think is a block doesn't fit neatly in a category. You can flip back to Chapter 4 for more thorough explanations of the categories.

- Losses (deaths, moves, missed experiences that you were looking forward to, friends moving away, etc.)
- Intense moments of fear (fear for your own safety or someone else's)
- Abuse or neglect (physical, emotional, or sexual abuse; not having your emotional needs met; worrying that your physical needs like food, shelter, and clothing wouldn't be met or actually not having them met)
- Family crises (prolonged illness, divorce, medical crisis)
- Seasons of depression and/or anxiety (for yourself or someone whose depression/anxiety negatively impacted you)

Step 2 - Lay out the timeline
You can imagine your timeline like taking your Grief Tower and laying it down on its side. Arrange the blocks you've written down into chronological order. Some blocks may not be moments, but rather childhood themes, and thus don't fit in chronological order. Some people like to put these blocks in a

different area of the paper, apart from the rest of the timeline. Others prefer to put them in their timeline in the timeframe when it felt most impactful. Some people like to use a journal for this; others prefer to use rolled out butcher paper, a large poster, or even sticky notes. You can just write the words, or you can draw a diagram with a shape around each block and lines connecting them. (See Example A)

EXAMPLE A

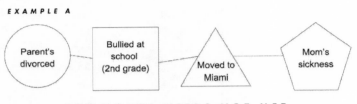

EMOTIONAL NEEDS NOT MET

Step 3 - Reflect
Step back, look at your Grief Tower Timeline, and take a deep breath. Pay attention to the emotions you're feeling and the thoughts you're thinking. Are you surprised to see how many blocks there are? What emotions are you feeling? Do you notice any patterns?

Step 4 - Add emotions
Using an emotions list or chart that can be found through a web search, ask yourself which two emotions you remember feeling during each block or experience. Then write those two emotion words under each block on your Grief Tower Timeline. (See example B.)

This will likely still be more of an intellectual process than an emotional process. We'll spend time going back and processing each of the blocks emotionally, so it's okay if this step feels more methodical than emotional. If you're feeling an emotional response, notice it and continue through this step, keeping in mind the indicators from Chapter 3 that you should press pause and doing so if needed.

When you've listed all of the emotions, step back. Are there patterns? Are there one or two emotions that seem to show up a lot? Does that surprise you?

EXAMPLE B

E M O T I O N A L   N E E D S   N O T   M E T

UNSTACKING THE BLOCKS

Discovering Narratives

Exercise #1:
For each of the blocks on your Grief Tower Timeline, see if there is a narrative about yourself, relationships, or spirituality that came out of that block. Write each one down. You may find that the same narrative keeps repeating. Underline that narrative every time it seems to be reinforced by another block on your timeline. Then, consider how your view of the world influenced how you perceived the blocks on your timeline.

Exercise #2:
For narratives about yourself, write both the helpful and harmful versions. Do you tend to be more controlling of yourself or more controlling of others? (Refer to Chapter 9 for examples.)

Exercise #3:
Are there any narratives that feel difficult to let go of because they've been so ingrained in your identity? What might happen if you live into that narrative for the next 10 years (physically, emotionally, relationally)?

Exercise #4:
For each narrative, write a combating narrative. Consider writing your combating narratives in a form that can be displayed.

- Sticky notes on a mirror
- A list on your fridge
- Hand-lettered artwork
- Digital art printouts

PROCESSING

Your Grief Tower Timeline has now become your processing to-do list. You'll go through each block one by one, using the following process for each. There is no prescribed order you should do this in, and you can start anywhere on your timeline.

Grief processing simply brings forward the unconscious, tucked away, grief-inducing experiences and gives intentional thought to them while also allowing for feeling the emotions that may have been long suppressed.

Often those experiences are stored in our more instinctual, back part of our brain. When they live there, they can be triggered by similar events, experiences, sights, sounds, or smells. In that space, they aren't being reasoned through by our front, thinking brain; they are being reacted to by our back, instinctual brain. When we process, we are analyzing that memory with our front brain and, in a sense, neutralizing the power that memory has in the back brain.

You'll do this by using the following Processing Questions as a framework, along with a Processing Activity. The Processing Questions are listed below for easy reference and then expounded upon thereafter.

Processing Questions

- What emotions did I feel in that season or situation?
- What made that feel so hard?
- How did it feel in my body?
- What coping skills did I use to get through that season or event?
- What narratives came out of those blocks?
- How have those narratives influenced my actions?
- What do I want to take from this experience, and what do I want to leave behind?
- If I haven't talked about this out loud with anyone, who is one safe person I can tell?

What emotions did I feel in that season or situation?

When you created your timeline, you wrote down two emotion words. These are the primary emotions. What you are answering now is, "And what else?" Answering that question allows you to dig deeper into your emotional response to the block.

What made that feel so hard?

What makes it feel so hard is that sublayer of less obvious losses. The obvious grief experience is just the tip of the iceberg. It's not just the thing that happened; it's also the:

- Loss of being known
- Loss of routine
- Loss of comfort
- Loss of feeling safe
- Loss of closure

- Loss of having that person to call when you're lonely
- Loss of intimacy
- Loss of your status
- Loss of that thing you thought you'd experience
- Loss of a place that feels homey

Naming the hidden losses allows us to begin to understand the emotions we felt – or to feel them deeply for the first time.

How did it feel in my body?
Do you remember feeling tense? Sick to your stomach? So tired? It wasn't until I was processing through my own grief that I realized that a stomach ache always accompanied difficult events. Now, I pay attention to that particular type of stomach ache, knowing that it is a physical reaction to emotional distress. Until processing, I hadn't noted it as a sign of experiencing something emotionally difficult.

Perhaps for you it is tight muscles, headaches/migraines, restlessness, a racing heart, a clenched jaw, or another symptom.

What coping skills did I use to get through that season or event?
Think about your actions around that event. What did you do to cope with it? You may want to flip back to the examples of coping skills in Chapter 5. What unhealthy ways did you cope? What healthy ways did you cope? How have those patterns continued since then? In what ways have they been healthy or harmful for you and the people around you?

Thinking about the healthy ways that you coped during those difficult times is just as helpful as acknowledging the unhealthy ways. You are then able to be intentional about leaning into those healthy skills and can catch yourself when you begin to shift to the unhealthy ones.

What narratives came out of those blocks?

Think about what that hard experience made you think or believe about yourself, the world, relationships, or spirituality. In other words, what did you begin to tell yourself?

How have those narratives influenced my actions?

As you've lived out that narrative, how has it impacted your decisions? The way you interact with people? The way you talk to yourself? The way you approach spirituality?

What do I want to take from this experience, and what do I want to leave behind?

We'll explore this further in the next chapter. What is something positive that came from this season or event? It could simply be, "I learned that I can make it through something very difficult." What is something that you'd like to leave behind? Perhaps it is an action or thought process that you developed that hasn't served you well or that you realize will be harmful going forward.

If I haven't talked about this out loud with anyone, who is one safe person I can tell?

Create a list of people in your life who have proven to be emotionally safe people. These are people who have validated your emotions, who know how to comfort you, and who will keep what you share in confidence. Consider asking them if you can share your Grief Tower Timeline with them. If you don't have anyone filling this role for you, finding a counselor can be a great way to get this support while you build a community of safe people around you.

PROCESSING ACTIVITIES

Processing can happen using a number of different methods. The only requirement is that you're doing something that accesses both sides of your brain. Doing this processing work will take time, so read through the ideas and take note of which you'd like to try.

Art Processing

Art processing is one of the most effective ways to process grief blocks because it engages both sides of the brain. Art processing can be structured, such as drawing something that represents a specific emotion or experience, or it can simply be thinking through the Processing Questions below while coloring mindlessly.

Other ideas are:

- Creating an artistic representation of what the experience felt like
- Putting together a collage of words and images that represent that block
- Drawing a self-portrait of you at the age you were during that block
- Drawing with shapes (search "shape art doodles" on Pinterest for some great ideas)

Nature Processing

Nature processing simply involves getting outside with the purpose of thinking through the blocks on your timeline and answering the Processing Questions. This could be going for a hike, fishing, sitting on the beach, laying on a blanket in the grass, or anything else that leaves you free to think intentionally. Often being outside brings a sense of calm and clarity that can help with processing. I have talked with many people who enjoy camping as a way to take intentional time in nature for the purpose of unstacking their Grief Tower.

Verbal Processing

Verbal processing simply means talking through the questions and timeline blocks with a trusted friend or family member. This may seem like an obvious form of processing, but I write it here so that you are aware that, although it's not the only way to process, it is one form of processing. If you choose to verbally process with someone, it is helpful to inform them of what you are doing and how you would like them to interact. You can, perhaps, even have them read this book so that they understand the process.

Written Processing

Use the Processing Questions as journaling prompts to jump-start your writing. There are many ways you can be creative when journaling. Some ideas could be writing a letter to someone that you'll never send, writing out prayers, writing your story in third person, or using bullet points. One of the most commonly chosen written processing methods with our clients is writing a letter to your past self. Here are some prompts to use if you choose to try that method.

- Are there any feelings you had at the time that you didn't understand? Tell Past You what those were, and invite your past self to experience those feelings.
- Were you denying yourself any emotions at that time? Acknowledge those emotions in Past You, and tell your younger self that it makes sense that you felt that way.
- How do you wish you had been comforted in that time? Use those words to comfort Past You.
- Give grace to Past You and remind your past self that you did your best.
- Looking back, what things are you proud you did during that time? Encourage Past You in those things.
- Tell Past You about where you are now and what there is to look forward to.

Exercise Processing

Processing through grief while doing a physical activity can be a helpful combination, but it must be intentional. Exercising with headphones in, while listening to an audiobook, or while watching television can be a great stress reliever, but it is not grief processing. When using exercise to process grief, it's important to go in with the specific block that you'd like to ponder and work through. As you exercise, imagine yourself back in the season or situation as best you can. Then think through the Processing Questions for that block. Some ideas are running, shooting basketballs in a hoop, biking, weight lifting, swimming, or dancing.

Cozy Processing

Some of us are very tactile and need to process in an environment that feels cozy. You may consider setting up a processing space that features elements that delight your senses.

Some examples include:

- Candles
- A soft blanket
- Quiet music or calm background sounds
- A comfy chair
- Twinkle lights
- Colorful decor
- A cup of your favorite coffee or tea
- Diffuser with oils or other scents

Combining

Of course, many of these methods of processing can be combined. You can go for a hike in nature while verbally processing with a friend. You can journal or do art in your cozy processing space. There are many methods even beyond the examples in this chapter. I know people who process through writing poetry or song lyrics about their experiences, by writing books, through dancing, cooking, or gardening.

The point is, there are many ways to process, and it's important to find what feels the best to you and to do it intentionally. If you're anything like me, you may need variety in your processing, so having this list of options to look back on can be helpful as you tackle processing through your Grief Tower. If you're having trouble feeling emotion while using these processing activities, consider one of the suggestions from Chapter 8.

Creating your Grief Tower Timeline and listing emotions for each block are steps you can do in a relatively short period of time. We host weekend Unstacking Retreats where participants do these two steps in one afternoon. The next step of processing each block, however, may take weeks or even months.

During the Unstacking Retreat, we encourage participants to focus on one or two blocks that they feel carry the most weight in their life. They work through the Processing Questions and a Processing Activity for each over the span of one day. Then they can slowly work through the other blocks on their tower in the coming weeks and months. The Unstacking Method is not a quick fix but rather a systematic guide for gently processing each block one by one.

You have a few options in this moment:

- Continue reading this book and come back to this chapter when you have time set aside and are ready to begin unstacking.
- Do the four steps of writing out your Grief Tower Timeline and then continue through the book, coming back to the processing part when you're ready.
- Write out your Grief Tower Timeline, and choose just one block to practice going through the Processing Questions and a Processing Activity before you continue on through this book. If you're a practitioner learning how to use this method with those you support, I

would encourage you to try this process of thinking about a Grief Tower block of your own before using the Unstacking Method with clients.

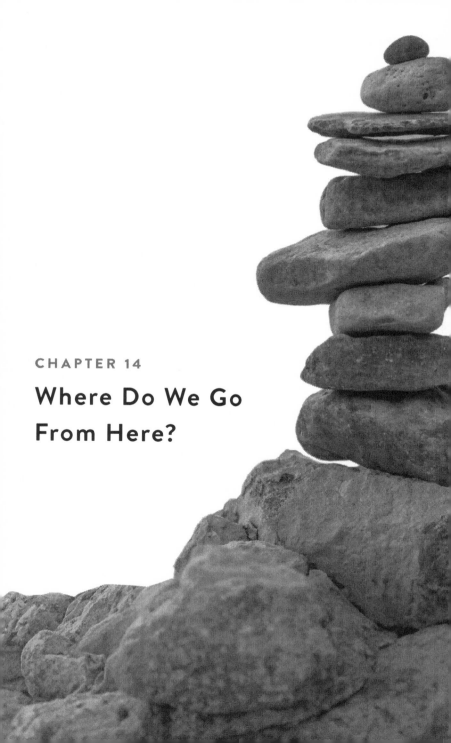

CHAPTER 14

Where Do We Go
From Here?

"When we truly understand the impact that trauma had on us, self-judgment will be replaced with a profound sense of self-compassion."

— Jerry Henderson

However you have coped with your Grief Tower and whatever narratives came out of your blocks, they helped you to survive. You may be looking at your Grief Tower and wondering how you let yourself live out past hurt in the present in ways that have been unhealthy for you or harmful for people in your life. Maybe you're kicking yourself for not even noticing these patterns until now.

Or perhaps you're feeling the normal grief that comes with letting some things go that were a part of you for so long. As you unstack and heal, part of the grief will be saying goodbye to the version of yourself who lived a life influenced by your grief blocks. It makes sense that letting that go would feel hard.

First and foremost, I want you to acknowledge and affirm the emotions that come when you think about moving forward with an unstacked tower.

If you're feeling uneasy, sad, or hesitant to let go of your Grief Tower, explore why that might be. What makes that feel hard to do? What parts of your tower are healthy and can and should be carried forward with you? Why might you choose to leave the other parts behind?

Perhaps you're feeling sad and angry as you realize the weight and impact of the hard things on your tower. Maybe this is the first time you've explored why those things felt so hard. Psychologist Dr. Caroline Leaf says, "As you heal you will grieve the moments you missed out on, how certain people failed you, and what your younger self deserved but didn't get. It's ok to be sad and angry."[44]

---

44 Leaf, Caroline [@drcarolineleaf]. (2023, August).

You might be feeling guilt or embarrassment for how you've lived life out of your Grief Tower. Recognize that you did the best you could with the information and resources (internal and external) that you had. Commend yourself for surviving, and lean into the hope of moving forward in healthier ways.

If you're feeling hope and relief realizing that there is another way forward than the road you've been walking, press into that.

Processing past grief is a complex process with so many layers, and the mixed emotions that often come with moving forward are part of that complexity.

AN HONORABLE DISCHARGE

Your tower may have served you in ways that you don't need anymore. Perhaps your narratives gave you protection that you felt you needed, or your coping methods met the needs that weren't being met by loving relationships. Maybe your narrative about relationships gave you a sense of control that seemed to keep anxiety at bay, or your narrative about yourself helped you exchange fear for anger.

Whether it was ultimately good or not, you received something from your narratives and coping skills, or they wouldn't have stuck with you like a static-charged blanket. You kept going back to them for a reason, and that reason is worth acknowledging.

Look back through your timeline, your narratives, and your coping patterns. What did each of them make you feel? What did you gain from them?

Whatever they gave you, it likely wasn't inherently bad. Protection, freedom, control, safety – these can be good and healthy things.

At the risk of sounding cheesy, I want you to thank yourself for working so hard to put those things into place. Thank yourself for doing what it took to keep you alive. Thank yourself

for continuing to step forward, even if those steps look coun-
terproductive in hindsight.

It's time to give those narratives and coping strategies an
honorable discharge:

"Thank you for what you did. I can take it from here."

WHAT HAVE YOU GAINED?

I think back to myself as a teenage girl with a fast-stacking
Grief Tower. I remember the young woman sobbing on the
bathroom floor of the law office after a second miscarriage.
I grieve for her and all that she had to go through. And if I
could sit with her in those moments, I would hold her and
tell her gently, "Don't lose hope. There will be meaning in all
of this." The only reason I can sit here writing this book, the
reason I have built companies that provide emotional health
and grief processing resources that have helped thousands,
the only reason I am who I am is because my life wasn't easy.
If it had been, I wouldn't be living the life I'm living now. There
were years when the grieving outweighed the meaning and I
thought my Grief Tower would swallow me up. But the work
of processing my tower strengthened the meaning behind it
and was a catalyst in healing from it.

We don't become resilient by never going through hard
things. We become resilient by pushing through the hard and
coming out the other side. The fact that you have lived through
the blocks on your Grief Tower is a testament to your strength,
tenacity, and perseverance.

Post Traumatic Growth (PTG) is a research-based theory that
explains transformative growth after trauma. Researchers
have found that people who experience PTG "develop new
understandings of themselves, the world they live in, how to
relate to other people, the kind of future they might have and

a better understanding of how to live life."[45] Post Traumatic Growth is measured in five areas:

1. Changes in how they relate to other people
2. Recognition of new opportunities, priorities, or pathways in life
3. Greater appreciation for the value of one's own life and life in general
4. Recognition of one's own strengths
5. Spiritual or existential development

For some people, PTG happens naturally. Perhaps you're reading this book realizing just how much your Grief Tower has organically spurred growth in each of the areas above.

But even if not, studies have shown that PTG can be fostered through many of the avenues we've already been exploring in this book:

1. Education – discovering core belief systems that came out of our trauma and intentionally deciding which ones to carry into the future with you.
2. Emotional regulation – learning to listen to our emotions and have self-control over our behaviors as we feel and express emotion.
3. Disclosure – having someone you can talk to about the hard things that have happened who listens well and provides support.
4. Narrative development – creating a new, accurate story about the trauma and how it can positively impact the future. ("That was extremely difficult, but it gave me the ability to be more empathetic toward others going through something similar" or "If that hadn't

---

45 Collier, L. (2016). Growth after trauma. *Monitor on Psychology*, *47*(10). https://www.apa.org/monitor/2016/11/growth-trauma

happened, I never would have been forced to deal with
some other harmful behaviors that could have resulted
in outcomes far worse.")

5. Service – finding ways to serve others, especially
serving others with strengths and skills that you
learned or grew in because of the hard things you
experienced.[46]

Unstacking your Grief Tower is a process of using that
unstacked tower of past hardships to propel you forward into
a future that is even more free, resilient, and meaningful than
what it would have been if you'd never had a Grief Tower in
the first place.

FORGIVENESS

*"I am a soul who likes the concept of forgiveness . . . until I am
a hurting soul who doesn't."*

– Lysa TerKeurst

It is likely that being curious about your Grief Tower has led you
to discover or remember people who intentionally or uninten-
tionally hurt you. Perhaps it has made you realize that part of
the reason those hard things felt so hard is because of the lack
of care you received from the people who should have been
nurturing you and holding you tight in your hardest moments.

A key piece of unstacking your tower is forgiving those who
were directly or indirectly responsible for the blocks on there.
As Lysa TerKeurst says in her book, *Forgiving What You Can't
Forget*, "Staying here, blaming them, and forever defining your

---

46 Tedeschi, R. (2020). Growth after trauma. *Harvard Business Review.* https://
hbr.org/2020/07/growth-after-trauma

life by what they did will only increase the pain. Worse, it will keep projecting out onto others. The more our pain consumes us, the more it will control us. And sadly, it's those who least deserve to be hurt whom our unresolved pain will hurt the most."[47]

Forgiveness may be something that takes time. It may be something that you mentally choose to do with your brain before your heart follows along. Healing is slow, and forgiveness is likely to be a gradual process. Allow yourself the time and space to wrestle with the concept without feeling guilt over forgiveness not coming quickly or easily.

Forgiving isn't forgetting what happened, deciding that it wasn't that bad, or making excuses for why they acted in that way. Instead, it's "an intentional decision to let go of resentment and anger."[48] That intentional decision doesn't have to *feel* like anything right away. It can be an entirely left-brained process until your right brain eventually catches up and decides to believe it emotionally as well.

Forgiveness also does not mean that you grant the person physical or emotional access to your life. If they haven't shown that they are trustworthy, that access should still be limited. Access and forgiveness don't always go hand in hand.

A study on the impact of forgiveness on mental health showed clear correlation between forgiveness and measures of mental health and well-being on a clinical scale. Those who practiced intentional forgiveness experienced lower levels of depression and anxiety and higher levels of self-esteem. Remaining hostile and withholding forgiveness was linked to negative effects on cardiovascular health.

47 TerKeurst, L. (2020). *Forgiving what you can't forget.* Thomas Nelson.

48 Mayo Clinic. (2022). *Forgiveness: Letting go of grudges and bitterness.* Retrieved September 4, 2023 from https://www.mayoclinic.org/healthy-lifestyle/adult-health/in-depth/forgiveness/art-20047692#:~:text=What%20is%20forgiveness%3F,might%20always%20be%20with%20you.

And here's where it gets really interesting: both the positive effects of forgiveness and the negative effects of unforgiveness are amplified when it involves forgiving yourself.[49] In other words, forgiving yourself for something you've done can have powerfully positive effects on your physical and mental well-being – even more so than extending forgiveness to someone who wronged you.

Whether the unstacking process has uncovered feelings of hostility or resentment toward people who harmed you or toward yourself, carrying that forward will never lead to the healing that brings health and freedom into your life.

That said, forgiveness often takes time, energy, and support. This may be an area that could benefit from professional support such as a counselor or a forgiveness support group, which provides a group setting in which a facilitator guides participants through the process of working to forgive.

STRENGTHS

We don't need to be glad that the hard thing happened to acknowledge the strengths we gained from it. Looking at your Grief Tower Timeline, make a list of character traits, skills, and attributes that you wouldn't have to the extent that you do if you hadn't endured that difficult experience.

Perhaps you're more empathetic to others who are going through difficult times. Maybe you've developed an intense grit that gets you through long days and challenging work projects. You may be a more nurturing and sensitive parent. Or, maybe you're a more present and involved friend.

While unstacking is about looking at the unhelpful things we'd like to change, it's equally about searching for the strengths and

---

49 McCullough, M. E., & Witvliet, C. V. (2002). The psychology of forgiveness. *Handbook of positive psychology*, 2, 446-455.

positive attributes that we want to lean into as we learn to process our grief and move forward in healthier ways.

My Hope For You

I hope that your eyes are open to noticing when unhelpful narratives start to show themselves. I hope that you're quicker to recognize their unhelpfulness and to pull out a combating narrative to actively replace the harmful one.

I hope that you'll continue processing each block on your Grief Tower Timeline, giving yourself the time and space to feel the emotions deep within each of the blocks. I hope you'll explore new avenues for processing that you haven't tried before.

I hope that you'll take what you've learned to the people in your life. To love them well. To support them in hard times. To give them language if they're in the middle of a Grief Tower block experience and don't understand why it feels so hard. I hope you'll lead the children in your life to unstack their tower along the way by asking good questions and giving them space to feel emotion.

I pray that your life will be freer. That your relationships will be deeper. That your spiritual life will be richer. I pray that as you continue to unstack your Grief Tower, you'll feel lighter, fuller, and braver – knowing that your resilience has increased and the boulders you've been carrying have been gently set down, one by one.

I pray that you'll unstack the hard things as they come and that you'll thrive because you're no longer walking through life with a tall Grief Tower.

Exercise #1: What emotions come to mind as you think about unstacking your Grief Tower?

Exercise #2: What emotions come to mind as you think about living with an unstacked Grief Tower?

Exercise #3: What strengths have come out of your Grief Tower that will help you as you go through the unstacking process?

Exercise #4: What good things in your life, or strengths you have, wouldn't exist if some blocks on your Grief Tower hadn't been a part of your story?

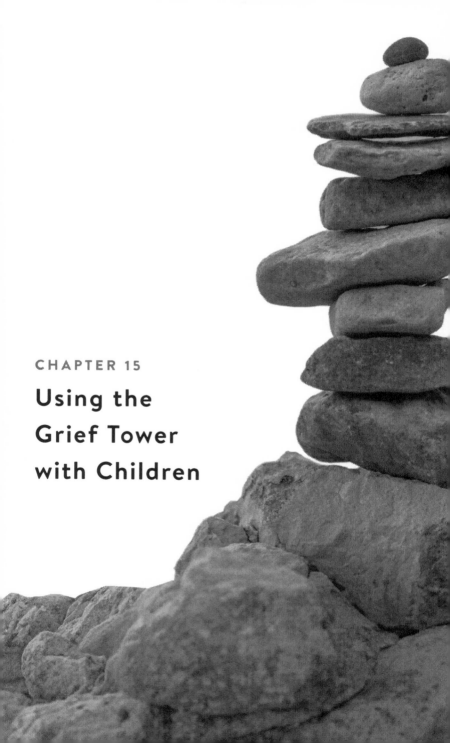

CHAPTER 15

Using the
Grief Tower
with Children

Now that you've done some of your own unstacking, I hope you can see what a valuable tool this can be. Perhaps you've thought, "Man, I wish I would have had this when I was younger." Or you've realized that your tower grew tall because you didn't have parents who provided a safe space for you to process hard things along the way.

You might even be thinking of the children in your life who already have extremely tall or toppled Grief Towers. One of the most encouraging things to remember is that research has shown that "Promoting protective factors is more effective in increasing resilience than reducing risk factors."[50]

This means that putting practices (like the unstacking methods we'll look at in this chapter) into place for children who have blocks on their Grief Tower is actually more resilience-building for children than if they were to never have Grief Tower blocks in the first place. Unstacking is an incredibly effective tool for both proactive and reactive care for children.

Unstacking with children can happen formally and informally, and this chapter will explain how to do both. Parents and those who regularly interact with children but without much one-on-one time, like teachers, will more often be engaging in informal unstacking, while practitioners such as counselors will often utilize the more formal approaches.

INFORMAL UNSTACKING

When we give children the opportunity and guidance to process grief in real time, it prevents difficult experiences from becoming long-term blocks on their Grief Tower, and it teaches them how to process difficult things that happen in their life. This habitual processing requires parents to be tuned

---

50 Kim, A., Kim, B., Lee, J., Lii, M., And Lee, S., Nam, S. (2013). Resilience: A meta-analytic approach. *Journal Of Counseling And Development, 91,* 269–79.

into their child's life and emotional needs and to have earned the child's trust as a safe space.

The good news is, trust is something that can be earned by repeatedly showing up as an emotionally safe space. When you do this, and when they courageously open up to you during difficult seasons, you prevent them from suppressing their grief. Instead of festering as a block on their tower, the grief gets processed and integrated into their life story.

Being a Safe Space

Showing up as a safe space begins with not giving what might seem like the natural response when children share a difficult emotion or experience with you. Our natural response is most commonly what I call a "shut down response." These responses do just that: they shut the child down.

We use these for a variety of reasons, but most often it's because we don't want the child to feel difficult emotions. It makes us uncomfortable or even distraught to watch a child experience sadness, display anger, or act in frustration. In order to make them – and us – feel better, we simultaneously shut down the emotion and the behavior.

That said, it's important to understand that being a safe space for emotions is just as important as having firm boundaries on behavior. You can show up as a safe space without permitting harmful or inappropriate behavior. In fact, part of being a truly safe space is teaching young people the importance of both through how we respond to their emotions.

I've worked with parents and those who work with children, such as teachers, who fall on all sides of the emotion vs. behavior spectrum. Those who want to be an ultra safe space for emotion might allow poor behavior to accompany difficult emotions in the name of being a "safe space." For example, a child is upset because they have to leave the park, and they begin hitting mom. The mom says, "It makes sense that you'd feel upset. Leaving the park is hard!" and then proceeds to get the child to the car while being hit the whole way there.

The acknowledgement of the emotions is a great start, but the mom never addressed the unacceptable behavior that cannot accompany the child's upset feeling. This lack of behavioral boundaries does not teach a child a healthy relationship with emotions of which the hallmark is, "I can feel this emotion, *and* I have to control how I act when I feel this emotion." Children learn this balance through adults allowing emotion while not allowing certain behavior to accompany that emotion. This skill is critical for children to learn throughout childhood in order to be emotionally healthy adults.

On the other end of the spectrum are those who have boundaries on both behavior and emotion. In their attempt to be a safe space, they say things like, "You can feel sad, but you need to go to your room until you stop crying." Instead of the crying being an opportunity for the adult to comfort and help the child process, it becomes a behavior the adult is trying to stop. More often than not, it's because the behavior makes the adult uncomfortable.

At the same time, parents or those who work with children know that sometimes the crying turns to shrieking or yelling. That's where the boundaries come in. We can say something like, "It's okay to cry when you're sad, but we don't scream like that in our classroom." For the adults who are tempted to put boundaries on both behaviors and emotions, it is important for you to think about acceptable behaviors to accompany difficult emotions. Here are some examples:

Sadness – Crying
Anger – Hitting a pillow or punching bag
Frustration – Saying "Ughh!"

Having clear indicators of when a child is expressing emotion in acceptable ways and when it turns to unacceptable behavior is important for making space for a child's emotions.

Of course, most of us fall somewhere in the middle of the examples given above, and it often depends on the moment and circumstance. The important thing is to be aware of our goals for responding to children's emotions.

Our goals should be to:

1. Teach them that no emotion is off-limits.
2. Show them that you will listen when they're ready to talk about what happened and help them understand their emotional response.
3. Teach them that they can feel an emotion *and* control how they act when they feel that emotion.

A great book for learning more about balancing boundaries with emotions is *Boundaries for Kids* by Dr. Henry Cloud and Dr. John Townsend.

Shut Down Reponses

When children share something difficult, it's tempting to respond with a "shut down" response because it's usually faster, it seems to turn off the emotional response, and we think we're doing the right thing by inserting our logic into their emotion. While all of the things we say may be true, shut down responses don't yield emotionally healthy children. They simply train children to give themselves shut down responses, and as we talked about in chapter 2, this leads to a tall Grief Tower because they go through life shutting down their emotions instead of ever processing them.

Most of the time when you're helping a child process their emotions, you're talking about small things that wouldn't necessarily be blocks on their Grief Tower whether or not you respond well. However, it is in these smaller moments that they are learning to see you as a safe space and are learning to process their emotions so that when the bigger hard things happen that would be blocks on their Grief Tower, they have the tools and experience in place to be able to process those things well.

These are some of the most common "Shut Down Responses":

Downplaying

When we downplay, we're implying that what they are sad or upset about isn't a big enough deal to warrant those emotions. This is particularly easy to do with little kids who often express emotion that seems to be more intense than the situation calls for.

Downplaying also shows up when we focus on what the child has to "be grateful for." If a child is feeling sad that they have to leave a friend's house, telling them that they should be grateful for the time they did have with their friends implies that they shouldn't feel sad because there's more to be grateful for.

Downplaying often shows up when we want to focus on the positive to help the child feel better. Unfortunately, focusing on the positive doesn't help the child to process the difficult event and thus, when bigger hard things happen that would be blocks on their Grief Tower, they don't get unstacked along the way.

Another common way downplaying shows up is when we respond with the phrase "at least." For example:

"I'm so sad my best friend is moving."
"At least you have your other friends!"

Defending

If the grief was caused by a decision you made (like moving, giving away a pet, choosing that school, etc), it's easy to defend your decision and explain why that was best for them. Unfortunately, this logic of "If they just knew there was a really good reason for this, they wouldn't feel _____" doesn't take away the feeling; it just shuts down the opportunity for them to process that feeling with you.

There is a time for an explanation of the decision-making process, but not before using the Safe Space Reponses we'll look at in a moment.

Comparing

Saying, "I've been there" – that is, empathizing when you truly have faced the same circumstances – can be helpful. However, comparing your experiences as better, worse, different, similar, or more intense in a moment when a child is needing to process their grief is not. For example, "When I was your age, we didn't even have ____ and I turned out fine. You really have it better than you think!"

Another way this shows up is comparing one grief experience to another. For example, "This isn't as hard as when ____ happened to you." You might be correct that it isn't as difficult, *and* both experiences need to be processed just the same.

Finally, comparing their experience to someone else's life somewhere in the world is also unhelpful. Saying things like, "I know this is hard, but at least it's not as bad as what ___ is going though!" doesn't take away the emotion; it just makes them feel ashamed for feeling it or keeps them from sharing it with you in the future.

Correcting

Correcting the facts in their story when they're expressing their grief is another common way we shut down emotional processing. In the moment when they're sharing why something felt difficult, the facts don't matter; their perspective does. It's their perspective that needs to be processed, not the facts. The likelihood is, the emotion wouldn't change even if they understood the facts perfectly. There's a time to narrate the truth for them, but it's not in that moment.

Safe Space Responses

Instead of shutting down a child's emotions, we can show up with responses that help them to feel heard, validated, and supported. Again, doing this with the small, seemingly insignificant things fosters a relationship in which they are more likely to come to you to process the bigger things instead of holding them in, and thus, not processing them.

When a child shares about or is clearly experiencing a difficult emotion, here's how we can show up as a safe space.

First...

Acknowledge

Acknowledge that they shared it with you and that you're glad they did. We've all been in situations where we share something emotionally vulnerable and leave wondering if we should have shared that. Dispelling that fear right away is an important place to begin. This is especially true for teenagers who are often very concerned about how they are perceived. You might say, "That was so brave of you to share that with me. I'm so glad you told me," or "Thanks for sharing that with me, I love that we can talk about these things," or "I'm sure this feels hard to talk about. I'm so glad you told me."

Affirm

Affirm that the emotion they are experiencing is valid and real. It may not make sense to you, or you may feel that it is more extreme than the situation warrants, but that doesn't mean that the emotion is wrong or doesn't make sense for them. As we discussed in Chapter 2, adults often shut down their own emotions because they learned growing up that their emotions weren't valid or worth paying attention to. We want to prevent this in children by saying, "It makes sense that you'd feel that way," or "That's a normal thing to feel when something like that happens," or "It's sad/frustrating/disappointing when ____."

Comfort

Comfort through connection. This could be offering a hug, spending some time together, or speaking some comforting words. You could ask, "Do you want to play a game?" or "Can I give you a hug?" or "Do you want to come sit by me?" or "Do you want to come be with me while I cook dinner/fold laundry/ run errands?"

Then...

Be curious by asking questions and simply listening

Sometimes, the best question is to repeat back the last thing they said.

For example, a child might say, "I'm sad because she said she didn't want to be my best friend anymore."

You respond with, *"Didn't want to be your best friend anymore?"*

"Yeah. She said she's best friends with this other girl now and that she can't have two best friends."

Asking a question that repeats back the last thing the child said will often encourage the child to continue the conversation, sharing more information.

Other good questions to ask are:

- "What did that feel like for you?"
- "I've never been in that situation. Can you tell me what it's been like for you?"
- "What made that feel so hard?"
- "How can I show that I love you right now?"
- "When you think back on that hard season, how do you feel? How does your body feel?"
- "Have you ever felt like this before?"
- "Do you want to know more about [what happened, why we made that decision, why that was important, etc.]?"

These skills can help a child's emotions to be processed in real time. When they are able to express their grievances both big and small to a safe person, they learn to trust that they can do that in the future. This prevents grief from being suppressed because they feel there is no safe outlet.

We can prevent a growing Grief Tower by learning and applying these skills with children from an early age. While the language you use might shift, these methods are just as important and effective for a five-year-old as they are for a teenager or adult. We never grow out of needing people in our life who offer Safe Space Responses instead of shutting us down.

FORMAL UNSTACKING

While the same Safe Space skills are also important for formal unstacking, a more direct approach to unstacking can be used in the counseling room, by social workers, by pastoral counselors, or even parents helping their children process stacked grief blocks from the past.

Appropriate Contexts for Unstacking

One of the great things about the Grief Tower concept is that it creates a visual aid that can be helpful for inviting children or teens to talk about hard things that have happened. These formal methods should only be used in contexts where there is full focused attention on the child or teen, where confidentiality can be maintained, and where trust has already been built. For example, these tools could be very helpful for a school counselor to work through with a student who has been coming to her office for regular care.

It would, however, be unwise for a teacher to use any of the following tools in a classroom setting where there are peers around and where their attention cannot be fully focused on one child. There may be contexts in which these could be used in a group setting (such as group therapy), but the group should be gathered for that purpose, as opposed to this being done nonchalantly within an established group that was not intended for grief processing, such as a classroom, Sunday school, or other extracurricular activity.

Knowing When to Pause

Children will have various levels of tolerance for how much processing they can handle, and before you begin unstacking with children, it's important to know how to do so in healthy ways. The most important factor is knowing when they have reached their emotional limit and it's time to pause and stop processing or shift directions. Dan Siegel, a Clinical Professor of Psychiatry, calls this limit the "Window of Tolerance." It's the amount of exposure a child can handle before they become hyper-aroused or hypo-aroused.

As you spend more time with a child building trust and teaching them to process their blocks, ideally that window of tolerance will grow and they'll be able to do more and more processing. It is critical, however, that we don't push them past what they are currently able to do, and that requires looking for signs that they have moved outside their window of tolerance.

Moving outside the window of tolerance activates the fight-or-flight response, and their brain and body respond accordingly. This can look like hyper-arousal, when our responses excessively increase, or hypo-arousal, when our responses excessively decrease.

Hyper-arousal when processing grief can look like:

- Difficulty concentrating
- Irritability
- Anger and angry outbursts
- Panic
- Frantically looking around the room or at the door
- Sudden fidgeting
- Constant anxiety

- Being easily scared or startled
- Self-destructive behavior

Hypo-arousal when processing grief can look like:

- Flat affect
- Inability to speak
- Blank stare
- Sudden exhaustion
- Shutting down[51]

If you notice any of these responses when talking about the Grief Tower with a child or teen, it's important to stop immediately. This is their body's way of telling you that it is too much for them, and pushing them at this point would be unproductive at best and harmful at worst.

If a child or teen exhibits signs that the conversation has gone past their window of tolerance, it's important to get them moving back to a regulated state, or as Siegel calls it, the "river of wellbeing."

Here are some basic methods for doing this:

- Breathing exercises
- Taking a drink of water – drinking from a straw can be especially helpful
- Squeezing a stress ball or playing with a fidget toy
- Coloring while listening to music
- 5-4-3-2-1 method (5 things they can see, 4 they can feel, 3 they can hear, 2 they can smell or imagine smelling, and 1 they can taste or imagine tasting)

---

51 Jersey Psychology and Wellbeing Service. (2020). The window of tolerance: Supporting the wellbeing of children and young people (Information and ideas for families and schools reconnecting after lockdown) https://www.gov.je/ SiteCollectionDocuments/Education/ID%20The%20Window%20of%20 Tolerance%2020%2006%2016.pdf

- Playing in a sensory bin (a bin filled with objects and a base substance such as sand, pebbles, or dry rice or beans)
- Laying under a weighted blanket

Once the child or teen is regulated, ask if they want to keep talking about their blocks or they want to be done. Respect their decision if they choose to be done processing. The next time you have the opportunity to talk with them about their Grief Tower blocks, consider starting with a different block and allowing them to choose which block to talk about next.

A helpful component of the Unstacking Method is that you're able to look at one block at a time. This means that while one block may have pushed the child or teen outside of their window of tolerance, a different block may not do that. It also means that we can set those other blocks aside until their window of tolerance has grown a bit, which can happen through increased trust and becoming more comfortable with processing emotions.

STEP 1 - INTRODUCING THE GRIEF TOWER

Introducing the Concept
For all of the activities outlined in this chapter, a visual introduction is a helpful start. Here are a couple of options:

Stacking the Tower
Using either blocks or rocks, explain explain to the child or teen that these represent hard things that happen in life. Share that we all have hard things that happen and that when we don't talk about these things with a safe person, they stack up, and eventually our tower will come crashing down.

As you explain this, stack up a tower of rocks or blocks, giving examples of hard things that could be blocks on the Grief Tower. You may start by asking the child, "What sorts of things might stack on the Grief Tower?" As you offer additional examples, be mindful not to give details or descriptors but instead vague examples that will bring forth memories in the children who have had similar experiences. What we're trying to do is to help them identify things that have happened in their life that would be considered a "block" on their Grief Tower without putting frightening ideas in their mind of things that *could* happen.

Here are some examples:

- Losing a pet
- Moving to a new house
- Hearing yelling in your home
- Being hurt by an adult you trusted
- Feeling unsafe
- A car accident
- Experiencing something scary
- An adult doing or saying things that made you feel uncomfortable
- Being bullied
- Losing a loved one
- A sibling moving away
- A parent getting very sick
- Parents getting divorced
- Not living with both parents anymore

Reading *My Tower is Tumbling!*

Marci Reneé wrote a book based on the Grief Tower Model called *My Tower is Tumbling!* This fabulously illustrated book follows a boy as he experiences various losses and collects rocks for each loss that he then carries with him.

Reading this book is a great way to introduce the Grief Tower concept and to get children thinking about the "rocks" they've been carrying. A standard version and a faith-based version are available on Amazon and Kindle. Both include a discussion guide at the end of the book.

Now that they have a visual in their mind, you can move on to one of the activities listed in Step 2.

STEP 2 - IDENTIFYING THEIR BLOCKS

Use one of the following options to help the child consider their own Grief Tower blocks.

GRIEF TOWER GAME
Materials needed: Traditional Jenga game or blocks that can be stacked.

Method:
- Set up the Jenga game on a table or floor.
- Take turns with the child pulling a block out of the tower, as in traditional Jenga. Each time a block is pulled out, invite them to share about a time they felt sad, worried, angry, afraid, frustrated, upset, or experienced something like one of the examples you gave before starting the game.

  When it's your turn, share a very vague, general example. For example, you might say, "One time my dog, whom I loved so much, died, and I was so sad" or "One time there was a big storm, and I was so scared that I hid under my bed." This is meant to encourage them to share because you're also sharing and/or to remind them of something that has happened to them that felt similar.
- Instead of placing the blocks on top of the Jenga tower, they will place it in front of them and create their own tower with their blocks. You'll do the same with the blocks you pull out of the tower.
- When the main tower collapses, talk about how the tower in front of them represents their Grief Tower. This is what grief looks like. It stacks up inside of us when we

don't talk about or process the things that have made
us feel sad, afraid, worried, or angry.
- Talk about the difference between the tower falling
over vs. purposefully deconstructing the tower. Which
feels better? Which is easier to clean up? Which makes
a bigger mess? Compare these answers to what happens
when someone's Grief Tower falls over vs. when they
intentionally unstack it.

Explain that you want to help them unstack their tower by
talking about the hard things that have happened in their life.
Acknowledge that unstacking the Grief Tower isn't very fun
and might feel really uncomfortable, but it is less painful and
destructive than letting it fall on its own. It is helpful to refer
back to this activity often to remind children that talking about
hard things is not easy, but if we don't, it will crash down like
the block tower, and that will feel so much worse.

COLLECTING ROCKS

Materials needed:
- River rocks
- Marker
- Bag or pillow case

Beginning with the examples in the "Introducing the Concept"
section, have the child write some hard things that they have
experienced on individual stones. Place them all in a bag or
pillowcase. Have the child pick it up, and ask questions like:
"What does it feel like?" "Could you play with friends while
you're holding this bag?" "Could you run very fast?"

Then you might say something like, "It's difficult to talk about
the hard things in the bag, but when we don't, we have to carry
them around with us."

Have the child pull out one stone at a time and go through
the processing questions with the child. Then have them do

one of the activities at the end of this chapter while thinking about that rock.

MAPPING OUT ROCKS
Materials needed:
- Paper
- Marker
- Scissors

After spending time with the child and talking about the types of hard things that would be on a Grief Tower, draw several circles or ovals of various sizes on a piece of paper.

Ask them to recall some hard things that have happened in their life.

You can either write their answers in each of the circles on the paper or have them spend time writing events in the circles. They may choose to put events they perceive to be bigger hardships in the bigger circles, and smaller hardships in the smaller circles.

Then have them cut out the circles.

Work with the child to arrange the circles in chronological order. The purpose is not to get it perfectly in order, but to gain a general understanding of the timeline of difficult events in their life.

Depending on the situation, you may involve the parents to help you arrange the events in chronological order.

GRIEF TOWER TIMELINE (FOR TEENS)
Materials Needed:
- Butcher paper or a roll of paper
- Markers, colored pencils, or crayons
- Emotions chart or feelings wheel (these can be found through a web search)

While some practitioners have used the Grief Tower Timeline with younger children, we've found that the other recommended methods in this chapter work best for children under age 12. The need to categorize events chronologically for the Grief Tower Timeline can be difficult for younger children.

To guide the teen through creating their Grief Tower Timeline:

Roll out the butcher paper on the ground or table. Give the teenager instructions for doing their own timeline and allow them ample time to create it. If they'd like, you can walk through it with them, or they can take it to a separate location to create it privately. In some settings, practitioners will assign the timeline creation as homework and then ask the teen to bring it with them to the next session to begin processing through the timeline.

The teenager's timeline should include:

- Losses (deaths, moves, missed experiences that they were looking forward to, friends moving away, etc.)
- Intense moments of fear (fear for their own safety or someone else's)
- Abuse or neglect (physical, emotional, or sexual abuse; not having their emotional needs met; worrying that their physical needs like food, shelter, and clothing wouldn't be met or actually not having them met)
- Family crises (prolonged illness, parent's divorce, medical crisis, etc.)
- Seasons of depression and/or anxiety (for themselves or someone whose depression/anxiety negatively impacted them)

Instructions to give the teen:

1. Draw blocks for anything that fits into the categories above.
2. Below each block, write two emotion words or draw emotion faces that describe your feelings around that event.

3. Circle which events felt the hardest.

Then talk about the importance of processing each block, and give them the options for doing so. Refer to the Processing Tools at the end of this chapter.

STEP 3 - PROCESSING TOOLS

All of the activity options in Step 2 create a list of Grief Tower blocks to be processed The purpose of that is to have a working list of the things that you should support the child or teen through processing.

As you begin processing, pay special attention to the "Knowing When to Pause" section in this chapter so that you don't push a child past their tolerance level for processing. If you are in a professional relationship with the child, you may push pause and then try to revisit that block again in your next session. If you are not in a professional role, then encourage the parent to follow up on that specific block by arranging for the child to meet with a counselor or psychologist.

The child or teen will process through their blocks by answering the Processing Questions and either simultaneously doing a Processing Activity or doing the activity after talking through the questions with you.

Processing Questions
1. What made that feel so hard?
2. What emotions did you feel?
3. How did it make your body feel?
4. What did it make you think or believe about (yourself, people, God, the world)?
5. What did you start to do differently after that happened?
6. Have you talked to anyone about this before?
7. How do you feel talking with me about it now?

These questions are meant to be a guide, not a script. Use them to converse with the child or teen and get them thinking about how the event made them feel and how it impacted them. The purpose of this is for their brain to begin processing the Grief Tower block and for them to begin noticing how it has impacted them. This left-brained process sets them up to move to one of the more right-brained activities below.

Processing Activities

STONE ART
Materials Needed:
- River rocks
- Paint or a paint pen
- Marker

Have them write the hard thing that happened on a stone. Then encourage them to pick colors and patterns that represent the emotions they were feeling when that hard thing happened.

Allow them to color their stone however they want to. Then ask them to share about the way they chose to color the stone.

SELF-PORTRAIT
Materials Needed:
- Paper
- Coloring utensils

Ask them to draw a full body self-portrait of how they felt during the hard thing that took place.

As they draw, you can prompt them by saying things like:

- Were their tears on her cheeks?
- Did his eyebrows scrunch because he felt tense?
- Are her hands closed into fists?
- Is he standing up straight or hunched over?

As you do this, you might act these things out so the child can visualize the concepts.

When they're finished, ask them to tell you about their picture.

EMOTIONS WEB

This activity is best for older children and teens.

Materials Needed:
- Paper
- Pencils, pens, or markers

Have them draw a circle in the center of the paper and write the event or experience that they're going to process in the middle of the circle.

Then have them draw a line from the center circle to another shape. In that shape they'll write an emotion word that they felt during that difficult event or experience. They'll continue to do this until they have several emotions listed. Encourage them to use different colors for the different emotions and to draw the size of the shape depending on how strongly they felt the emotion they're writing inside it.

After this, have them draw a line from each emotion circle to another shape. In this shape, they'll write the reasons why they felt that emotion.

This activity is good for those who tend to be more right-brained and lean toward feeling more than forming organized thoughts about the difficult thing that happened. This web can help them to find language that validates the big feelings they experienced.

WRITING A LETTER TO YOUR PAST SELF

This activity is best for older children and teens and is also presented in Chapter 13 for adults to use.

Invite them to write a letter to their past self in the moment or season when they were going through the difficult Grief Block.

Here are some prompts to get them thinking:

- Are there any feelings you had at the time that you didn't understand? Tell Past You what those were and welcome them to experience those feelings.
- Were you denying yourself any emotions at that time? Acknowledge those emotions in Past You and tell them that it makes sense that they would feel that way.
- How do you wish you had been comforted in that time? Use those words to comfort Past You.
- Give grace to Past You and remind them that they did their best.
- Looking back, what are you proud you did during that time? Encourage Past You in those things.
- Tell Past You about where you are now and what they have to look forward to.

Other processing methods could be:
- Coloring on paper or canvas some shapes, colors, and patterns that represent what the experience felt like
- Putting together a collage of words and/or images that represent that block
- Going into nature to talk or think through the processing questions
- Writing the story of what happened in the third person
- Doing stretching exercises while thinking through or talking through the processing questions

Again, with children we are introducing the concept, having a conversation using the processing questions, and then separately or simultaneously doing a processing activity that will aid in bringing both sides of their brain together to process the Grief Tower block.

As I discussed in the beginning of the chapter, the goal would be to help them to preventively and proactively unstack their tower as hard things come in their life. The same methods and activities could be used on an as-needed basis for new hardships that arise.

This doesn't mean that they'll never need to process that event again – they'll likely need to reexamine it when they've grown in wisdom, experience, and maturity. But intentionally unstacking along the way keeps it from being an unprocessed block that creates the environment for a tall and eventually crashing Grief Tower. It also is what helps them to be able to look back and feel that, while those things were difficult, they had supportive, nurturing adults in their life helping them through it.

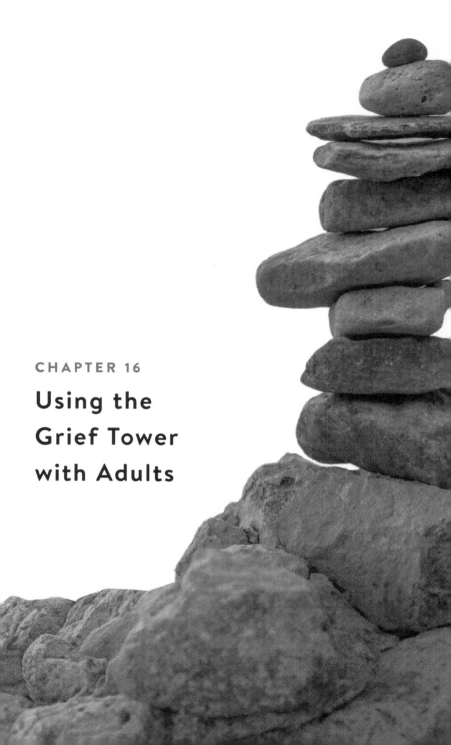

CHAPTER 16

Using the
Grief Tower
with Adults

The Grief Tower method can be a great tool for helping people to begin to process what has happened in their life and how it impacts them today. If you are a counselor, you might choose to use this tool in a more clinical manner. However, its use is not restricted to those with a clinical background, and it can be used by anyone – with limitation.

The primary limitation is to know when you need to "press pause" and encourage the person to seek services from a mental health professional. Many of the conversations suggested in this chapter are safe to have with a person or in a group where trust has been established. However, there may come a point where the direction of these conversations leads to a trauma response, and the individual should not proceed with the conversation.

Revisit the "Pushing Pause" section in Chapter 3 for indicators that it's time to take a break. If you notice any of the trauma responses listed there, refer to a mental health professional or, if you are that professional, give tools for regulating before reentering the conversation.

COUNSELORS/THERAPISTS

Counselors and therapists all around the world have found the Grief Tower Model to be a helpful way for them to engage with their clients. They've shared that clients seem to more easily grasp the importance of looking at past hardships and that they feel a sense of control because they can wrap their head around this method and its goals.

Here are some ways that counselors have used the Unstacking Method that may be helpful to you:

- Teach about the Grief Tower, and then work with the client to create their Grief Tower Timeline (either in the session or assigned as homework). Use subsequent sessions to work through one block at a time, keeping in mind that some blocks may require more than one session. In the sessions, focus on the processing questions and help them to dig into their narratives – identifying the unhelpful ones and helping them to create combating narratives. In between sessions, encourage them to try some of the ideas for naming and feeling emotions in Chapter 8 and/or the processing ideas in Chapter 13.

- Use their primary reason for seeking therapy to lead to the blocks on their Grief Tower. For example, if they came to you because they "just can't seem to stay in a relationship," invite them to be curious about Grief Tower blocks in their past that may have led to that belief. Work with them to create their Grief Tower Timeline for the purpose of investigating where that specific belief or pattern may have come from, and then work together to process those related blocks.

- Process current grief by using the Processing Questions and activity ideas in Chapter 13. Don't dig into past grief or create a Grief Tower Timeline, but instead, help them to balance coping (Chapter 5) with processing by working with them to help them learn their window of tolerance for how much processing vs. coping they can do at that time.

- Use the Processing Questions as a way to guide clients through talking about any difficult experience that they share with you.

COACHES

Coaching is typically differentiated from counseling in that coaching is future-oriented, action-focused, and works toward clear, measurable goals, while counseling is focused on the past with difficult-to-measure goals. There is significant room for nuance in those definitions, but if you are a coach, the Grief Tower Model can be helpful in guiding your clients toward meeting their goals.

- In career coaching, you might use the Grief Tower to uncover what's holding them back from moving toward their goals. Are there narratives holding them back? Unhealthy coping skills? As you work with them to create career goals, invite them to be curious about how hardships in their past might be informing their thoughts or actions about those goals. Sometimes it's as simple as asking good follow-up questions. For example, if they say, "I'm just not a very good leader. I can take direction, but I'm not cut out for leadership." Perhaps ask, "Is there something that happened that's making you think that way?" or "Did someone ever say or imply that?"

- Life coaching is where the Unstacking Method can be incredibly useful. As your client sets goals, one of the first steps toward meeting those goals should be looking at the internal barriers to meeting them. If those internal barriers are not noticed and processed, their goals will never be met. You may have them read this book or watch one of our workshops on Unstacking Your Grief Tower (www.unstackingco.com) and ask them to pay attention to anything that comes up for them that might hold them back from reaching their goals.

- Relationship coaching can use the Unstacking Method to pull out and focus on relational narratives. As you guide your client in developing healthy relationships, have them learn about the Unstacking Method so they can see if they can find relational patterns in their Grief Tower. Work together to create combating narratives that will help them to meet their relational goals.

FRIENDS

One of my favorite things about the Unstacking Method is how it allows us to show up for the people in our life when they're struggling with current grief or patterns that they can't seem to get out of. By understanding the Grief Tower Model, you're able to gently guide them through thinking about where these patterns, narratives, and emotions have come from in a way that eases them into processing. You might encourage them to learn about the Grief Tower for themselves, or you may just use your own knowledge to ask good questions (like the Processing Questions in Chapter 13), listen well, and notice with compassion patterns in their life that might be there because of hard things from their past.

IN CLOSING

Whether you picked up this book because you were curious about your own Grief Tower or so that you can help others unstack theirs, thank you for showing up. Thank you on behalf of your current and future relationships that will grow because of the work you put into finding and combating relational narratives. Thank you on behalf of the children in your life who need healthy adults to nurture and guide them through their hardships. Thank you on behalf of the ones you'll introduce to the Grief Tower so they can begin to engage in their own healing journey. And thank you on behalf of future you, who will benefit in ways you can't even begin to imagine because of the hard work you've put into unstacking your Grief Tower.

About Unstacking Company

Our mission at Unstacking Company is to unstack barriers to thriving by providing quality, research-based emotional health resources and education. We desire to see people move forward from their past into a healthier future, and we believe that the unstacking process is an important catalyst for this growth.

Unstacking Company serves:

INDIVIDUALS AND FAMILIES through online workshops, unstacking groups, worksheets, and more.

COACHES AND THERAPISTS through training on using the Grief Tower Methodology with clients.

SCHOOLS through staff training and curriculum on emotional health, resilience, and unstacking in a classroom setting.

CHURCHES through parent workshops, pastoral training, and speaking events.

(The *What Made That Feel So Hard? Bible Study Guide* that pairs with this book is available through Amazon. This resource is great for personal or group study.)

To learn more about Unstacking Company,
visit www.unstackingco.com

To book a training or speaking event,
email info@unstackingco.com

Follow @unstackingco on social media
to keep up with all of the new things we have underway!

Acknowledgments

This book has been in the back of my mind for a couple of years, but I knew the time wasn't quite right for it to be born. I held it loosely, awaiting the moment when I could jump headfirst into what I knew would be a taxing process.

I had a feeling the writing of this book would bring more sleepless nights and tears than any previous book I've written, and man, was I right. The number of times I awoke, scribbled illegible notes in the pad on my nightstand, and then gave up trying to go back to sleep, were countless. I could not have seen this project from start to finish without people in my corner who cheered me on to the finish line.

To my parents, Tony and Holly Freitas, who have continually cheered me on in every season of my life.

To my TCK Training Leadership Team – Elizabeth Smith, Jessi Bullis, and Tanya Crossman – thank you for emphatically giving me the green light on this project and for being a huge part of the development of the Grief Tower Methodology over the past years.

To Elizabeth Trotter, my wonderful editor, thank you for believing in this book and continually finding ways to make my long paragraphs shorter to make a challenging topic an easy read.

To Liz Stuart, thank you for the hours you spent helping me unscramble the content in my brain and get it onto the page in a logical flow. Your insights were invaluable.

To Catherine Plemmons, Elena Watson, Greta Owens, Alisha Garcia, Heather Panter, and Karen Wells – thank you for your friendship, encouragement, and enthusiasm during this process.

To Jillian Alexander, the friend I call in the highest highs and lowest lows. Thank you for being a sounding board, for believing in me, and for your wisdom that consistently influences both my work and life.

To my advisory team – Amy Young, Lisa Harrill, Julia Beaty, Hal Hamilton, and Jillian Alexander – thank you for journeying with me from the publishing of my first book until now. Without your faithfulness, insight, and excellent ideas, I wouldn't be where I am today.

To my TCK Training and Unstacking Company communities, thank you to those who have attended a workshop, received a debrief, worked through Unstacking Sessions, connected on social media, read a blog post, attended a training, sent an email, participated in our research, or simply cheered us on from afar. I am deeply grateful for you.

To my girls, Clara and Audrey, who keep me laughing and remind me why the hard work of unstacking is worth doing.

Finally, thank you to my wonderful husband, Aaron Wells, who is the very best teammate, a cheerleader in both work and life. Your unwavering love through my own unstacking process over the last fifteen years has been an anchor. While our Grief Towers have certainly grown during our decade of marriage, there's no one I'd rather do the work of unstacking with than you.

Made in the USA
Middletown, DE
10 April 2024

52845887R00123